THE

HUMAN

BEING

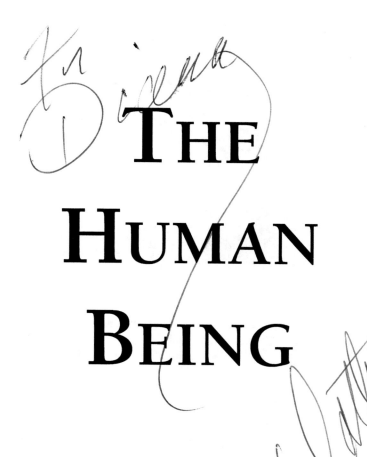

THE

HUMAN

BEING

by

NATHAN M. SHIPPEE

CYNTOMEDIA CORPORATION

Pittsburgh, PA

ISBN 1-58501-033-2

Nonfiction
© Copyright 2003 Nathan M. Shippee
All rights reserved
First Printing—2003
Library of Congress #2001096829

Request for information should be addressed to:

SterlingHouse Publisher, Inc.
436 Washington Avenue
Pittsburgh, PA 15218
www.sterlinghousepublisher.com

CeShore is an imprint of SterlingHouse Publisher, Inc.

SterlingHouse Publisher, Inc. is a company
of the CyntoMedia Corporation.

Cover design: Michelle S. Lenkner - SterlingHouse Publisher
Book Designer: N.J. McBeth

Printed in The United States of America

To

PATRICIA

THE HUMAN BEING

TABLE OF CONTENTS

Developing a definition for Human Being may provide our real "missing link." The Millennium has brought change. The new autonomy of the individual is prominent in these changes. The individual feels the change and seeks an identity within it.

One must ask, "Who am I?" The answer to that question is answered with another question, "Who do I think I am?" The answer is ...

I AM A HUMAN BEING

ALIENS WE

We were before
We shall be again
We are now
On the earth
But not of it.

A soul with a body
Visiting every region
As a ship the sea.

We are aliens, all
Self chosen to an aura
A luminous radiation
A distinctive atmosphere
Surrounding a selected source
Into which at conception
Each of us joined.

A time of life on earth
A soul with a body
A Being in human form
A Human Being
Aliens we.

Nathan M. Shippee

Have the courage to take your own thoughts seriously, for they will shape you.

— *Albert Einstein*

CHAPTER ONE

My Personal Journey

THE LEFT WING PLOWED THE RAIN-soaked field as mud blanketed the cabin window and the plane cart-wheeled, sheared left and broke apart. The right wing opened to the sky and I was flung out, still strapped to the seat, landing upright amidst the tornado-driven rain and hailstones.

The vision of the burning wreck was seen for the first time from afar. I was "Nathan" with all my senses, weightless and removed from all that was happening below me. There was a beautiful, azure blue environment of buoyancy, which was so peaceful and right that no words of mine have ever been able to describe it fully.

Then I was back with "myself" within the burning circle of debris and explosions. Then I was out again, several times, perhaps many times. This was repeated as Nathan moved higher away from the scene below. At one point, the pull from below being persistent, I said aloud to myself: "Okay, move your legs. If your legs move and you can walk, I'll stay with you. Otherwise I am not coming back again." I addressed myself as "you" and looked at my situation with detachment. Upon making the ultimatum, I regained focus, unbuckled my seatbelt, and stood up. Soon afterward I was working with others to help clear the burning area as rescue vehicles began to arrive.

Ambulances came and went. The driver of one small highway truck asked me if I needed a lift. The dark night and rain obscured the scene, but suddenly he saw my condition (bloodstained clothes, one shoe) and asked: "Were you on the plane?" No reply was needed. He helped me into his truck and drove back to the airport terminal. All the other vehicles had gone to area hospitals so we were the only one to arrive at the terminal.

Seemingly, people there were unaware of the crash. I walked in and the sight of me caused a commotion. Some good soul offered me a chair and before long I realized I was being taken to a nearby hospital.

The next morning, July 4, 1963, my first visitor, a kindly lady from the Red Cross, gave me shoes, pants, a shirt and shaving kit, which I took to the men's room. I shaved, dressed and walked out without ceremony to the railroad station where I boarded the next train to New York without a ticket, wallet or identification. When the conductor came by, I pointed to the headline in the New York Times newspaper describing the crash and told him that I had been on board the plane. I thought I was lucid but apparently he presumed that I was in shock and called ahead to have a State Trooper meet me and return me to my home in Greenwich, Connecticut.

I was deep in shock, and my body was so severely compacted by the crash that it was no longer functioning. My outward appearance was normal; internally all had come to a standstill. The doctor told my father of my problems and together they counseled me to try to stimulate my body functions by stimulating them mentally. It was my first experience with the concept of biofeedback, which subsequently became a principal part of my life experience and gave rise to my perception of the interaction of the contents and the container, and added a vital new dimension to my life.

My flight that morning on July 3 from Westchester Airport to Rochester, NY on Mohawk Airlines was a

Front page of *Rochester Times*, July 3, 1963.

business trip to conclude a merger negotiation. I was a highly active forty-four-year-old businessman in the midst of forming and operating companies in natural resources and international commerce. Suddenly, I found myself on the sidelines, and business was brought to a halt.

It was more than a year before I began to exercise decision-making activities, but the interim had not been a void. As I regained my body functions, I increased my mental awareness, until I realized that I was in control as a separate entity. My eyes did not see; I saw through my eyes. My fingers did not feel; I felt through my fingers. My feet did not walk; I directed my feet to move. I did not believe it when I saw it; I saw it when I believed it. This increasing transformation of consciousness occurred over the year and took the place of my entre-preneurial enterprises. I took time to read philosophy and attempted to relate my experience and its insights to deeper meanings of life. After reading the philosophers' densely-argued writings devoted to minute technical points of language and logic in the conventional fashion of academic philosophical study, I came to the conclu-sion that narrative was preferable to argument and that philosophy (as traditionally presented) fails to inform. Logic alone was inconclusive; it required clarification to complete concepts. René Descartes wrote: "I think, therefore I am." But he failed to say *what* I am. He should have completed the narrative with "I am to think."

With this thought in mind, I turned to writing philo-sophical essays on my own terms, with the basic require-ment of the logical clarification of thought and with the aim of confronting the deepest concerns of human life in an original and illuminating way.

Surviving the disastrous air crash was not the only turbulent experience I had, but it was the first in a civilian capacity and without preparation. Twenty years earlier I participated in three landings as a beach master during World War II, followed by the chaos of the revolution in China. These experiences, too, took their place in the shaping of my thoughts and philosophical expressions.

THERE WAS A WORLD WAR

I graduated from Rhode Island State College on a Thursday in 1941. I was a Second Lieutenant in uniform under my ceremonial cap and gown. June was still six months to December, but we knew then that war was imminent. On Saturday, a telegram came from the First Army District of New England with orders to report to Fort Benning, Georgia, to the Command and Staff College. I had been selected to represent the District for this assignment. On Tuesday, with over 200 others, we stood at attention in the auditorium when General Patton strode on stage and said, "Gentlemen, we are about to go to war. Your book days are past. You are here now to learn the art of survival under combat conditions. It will be like nothing you have ever experienced, and we shall try our best to make up for that in the next few weeks ahead." He was true to his word; they lost no time in getting started. The very next day we were crawling under barbed wire with fixed machine guns firing overhead. The next day we were digging foxholes (deep enough for tanks to move overhead). By Friday we were taking bayonet drill. Saturday night was time out downtown, where it was not unusual to end up with a brawl between the local National Guard unit and our Army group. The transition from college to combat was like a plunge into ice water: abrupt and at once breathtaking.

Fast-forward to December 7, 1941 with World War II now a reality. New services were being formed, reassignments were being made, and volunteers were called for. Beach landings and mobile ports were the new thing that appealed to me and I was reassigned to Fort Hamilton, New York as Company Commander of the Sixth Mobile Port Headquarters. Within a year, we were in the storm-tossed mid-Atlantic for a November landing in North Africa at Casablanca, where the French Free Forces offered no resistance, but the port was blocked with sunken ships alongside. It was a sleepless week of opening the area for troops and supplies to move inland before the German Army had time to react.

Then we had time to revise our plans and get ready for our turn at Italy. At Salerno, we had a different kind of reception. The German Army was dug in atop the hills surrounding the beachhead. Africa was far away, and we had only two-hour, limited air cover overhead. The German air corps flew down from Rome frequently, turning around Mt. Vesuvius before strafing and bombing our positions. It was touch-and-go for a week while we brought in equipment and troops to break out of the rim of hills and on into Naples. The importance of Salerno was its key to the success of the Normandy landings later. It pulled German forces away from the French Front, and weakened them on the Russian Front. It was a fiercely-contested engagement, among the worst of the war.

Southern France at Cavalier was a similar trial, but we were by then professionals in every respect. Pinned down for three days on and near the landing area, with Toulon and Marseilles held by the German Army, we made a decision to slip behind the German lines and go cross country to the mouth of the Rhone River and open up Port-du-Bouc to make an end-run up the river. With three machine-gun mounted jeeps we made the one-day trip in three days through the retreating German lines, mostly at night, and with the help of the Free French Allies. The plan worked. Toulon and Marseilles fell five days after we opened Port-du-Bouc, and the troops started moving up the Rhone River. Africa had been the end of the beginning. France was the beginning of the end. There was no letup, but the end was in sight. Thirty-six months in overseas combat was our life for as far as we could see ahead. When it was finally over, and we were on troop ships headed home, we were not ready to face a new life ahead.

The last night before landing in New York, we played poker all night and my long run of luck left me at the table. I bet my last dollar and when it went, I walked out on deck to watch the distant land lights ahead. After awhile, I reached into my pocket for the loose change there and flung it into the ocean as a gesture to the start of a new life ahead. There were plenty of us along the deck rail, and thoughts were shared of what we had done and what we were leaving behind. I recall, in particular, the thought about our fortunes. Did we ever think of not coming back? None of us ever did! Did we ever think of not winning the war? None of us ever did! Unwounded and victorious, we were all of one mind. We had met the best that had been thrown at us, and concluded that we could handle whatever was ahead.

Fast forward to December, 1945. The war is ended, but its memory lingers on. This young man in a suit and necktie was an inadequate image for a seasoned veteran with gold leafs and decorations from the American and French Governments for action in ground operations against the enemy in the liberation of the Port of Marseilles. The real problem in war is that you are pulled into the challenge of it. The return to civilian life for a youth who was devoid of any prior experience except war was more difficult than I had imagined it would be. After several attempts to match experience with job opportunities, I looked overseas for a challenge. My father-in-law was the Inspector General of Customs in China and the revolution there seemed to offer the opportunity I was looking for. Chase Bank, New York, planned to reopen its Shanghai branch. My application was accepted. Together with five others, I arrived in Shanghai in January, 1946 and remained until Shanghai fell to the Communists in 1948.

It was an immediate immersion into finance and business and a new and fascinating culture. The three years in China were as different from the three years in Africa and Europe as night and day. The war years were fought with real bullets; the revolution years were fought with silver bullets! In China, the procedure was "paved with money." A city would be surrounded by an advancing army which camped outside it for a week or more. Money would change hands, the gates would be opened and the city fell. This system was not without problems for many, but there were no bombings or frontal assaults which had fire-stormed the cities of Europe.

Shanghai was like Switzerland. Money poured in and out, in large sums and at great speed. Chinese businessmen are among the world's best, and I was quick to learn. China engaged foreigners for their top financial posts, including positions in the Postal Service and the Customs Service. My father-in-law had joined the Customs Service as a graduate from Dartmouth College in 1914 and had ascended to the top post of Inspector General. I therefore had the advantage of being an insider. I knew all that was happening on the political scene as one city after another fell to the advancing Communists, and in the financial markets as foreign exchange took flight.

The return to civilian life included the beginning of family life. My first child, a daughter, was born in Shanghai. As the Communists' gains continued, the fall of Shanghai became a certainty, and plans were made to evacuate. Bank records were packed up and shipped out. Personnel were reassigned, and a discreet arrangement was made with the City Fathers to let all but one of the bank managers out. One key executive remained behind as a hostage. The final episode, for me, was the transfer of the Government's gold reserves on board an American destroyer to Taiwan, and then embarkation on the American President Lines' *President Wilson* for the return to San Francisco.

WHERE AM I GOING?

My equilibrium was restored. Safely settled in Rhode Island with a family which grew to four children, I applied the China experience to entrepreneurial activities of my own, and prospered. Fifteen years of high energy activity was suddenly derailed with the air crash in 1963, which marked the dawn of a new outlook on life for me. The question was no longer *How to make a living?* but rather *How to make a life?*

In Southern France during World War II, I had met a philosopher, Denys de Columb, who engaged me in discussions and questions about "America" and how we would shape the world in the years to come. I do not recall all of his questions, but one observation he made stayed with me: "You do not fully understand something until you can reduce it to one word." Thirty-eight years later, when it came time to choose a title for the collection of philosophical essays about to be published, I recalled his statement and its challenge. There were ten essays, one each year beginning in 1968, each drawing on the cumulative life experiences of war, revolution, and the air crash. How could I reduce them all to one word? I spread out the ten essays and changed their sequence until a pattern emerged that spoke to me as the summary of human destiny, a concept that I had not been conscious of before. I rearranged the ten essays into a Table of Contents, and separated them into three sections. As I studied this, it dawned upon me that the essays were about the destiny of Human Beings. Human Beings are qualified Beings with a destiny of coming into Being.

Once my book, *Becoming: Coming into Being*, was published in 1979, the need to continue to express my thoughts was unabated and I began to think of a trilogy to complete the cycle of human destiny. To me, it was perfectly natural to turn to the dictionary for a definition of my next subject: *Human Being*. This initiated a 20-year contest with the dictionary companies over word meanings and common usage for even so basic a word as Human Being. My premise that **we become as we** *think* **and that who we** *think* **we are will determine our destiny** is the logical clarification of thought. Incidentally, the word "logic" is followed in the dictionary by the word "logjam," defined as "deadlock, a situation where something is blocked or at a standstill and is unable to progress." In a sense this book is about the forces that compete to dominate our thoughts and how the outcome will determine our destiny as Human Beings.

Every idea is an incitement. It offers itself for belief, and if believed, it is acted upon unless some other belief outweighs it. Many ideas grow better when transplanted into another mind than in the one where they sprang up.

— *Oliver Wendell Holmes*

CHAPTER TWO

THE PREMISE

WHAT MADE US HUMAN? CHARLES Darwin and Alfred Russell Wallace discussed this question over many years and the record of it remains in their correspondence. We, therefore, know that in spite of repeated appeals from Darwin, Wallace continued to believe that the otherwise ubiquitous and inescapable laws of natural selection did not act upon that most human essence, *the mind*. Wallace hoped that one day all would be explained by the discovery of new facts of a nature very different from any yet known to us.

What new facts have been discovered during the Twentieth Century? Erich Fromm, the German psychologist, identified one as transcendental awareness. Dobzbransky, the geneticist, went a step further when he wrote, "Man, this mysterious product of the world's evolution, may also be its protagonist and eventually its pilot."

Chapter IV, *Darwin Revisited*, explores the concept of the mind as more than Pilot. Professor Kenneth Miller,

Brown University Division of Biology & Medicine, author of Finding Darwin's God,[1] commenting on this concept set forth by the Author, wrote that he was

> "...happy to see how clearly you summarized the overwhelming evidence that Darwinian evolution had produced the "container," the human body. Your insistence that there is something more that makes us human ("our contents") is an interesting one, and I can see how you might regard it as the key to conflict resolution of this public issue."

New facts of a nature very different from any yet known to us, gave rise to the concept of the mind as more than "pilot, as captain." This new concept of the mind is expressed in the statement, *We become as we think*." This raises the question, *Who do we think we are?*" A change in our self-perception could change the course of our evolution. The concept raises the imperative of identification. We have the power to produce a new force, an incandescent force: the Human Being.

In Chapter III, *Through the Looking Glass*, the text opens with the famous line, "Who in the world am I? Ah, that's the great puzzle!" Coincidentally, the author of *Through the Looking Glass*, Lewis Carroll, was a contemporary of Darwin and Wallace in the 1850's. Darwin's focus was on "the container," while Carroll's was on the "contents." He wrote: "I have long supposed a Human Being to be capable of various states, and varying degrees of consciousness." These two opening chapters set forth the schism that has confronted us for the past one hundred and fifty years: Homo sapiens vs. Human Beings.

Chapters V through X examine the new facts of a very different nature from the one Wallace searched for, culminating in the Twenty-First Century discovery of the human genome. The June 26, 2000 joint announcement by the President of the United States and the British Prime Minister disclosing the mapping of the genome was transcendent. In the words of Dr. Francis Collins, Director of the National Human Research Institute, "We might have caught a glimpse of an Instruction Book previously known only to God." The Prime Minister said, "Mapping the genome has implications far surpassing even the discovery of antibiotics. The achievement carries humankind across a frontier and into a new era."

Walt Whitman anticipated this event a lifetime earlier in his "Democratic Vistas" when he wrote:

> "The rigor of mathematics has not been followed herein, but rather the pursuit of ideas. Ideas of the unknown and of unreality. The poems of life are great, but there must be poems of the purports of life, not only in itself, but beyond itself. Then will man indeed confront nature, and confront time and space, and take his rightful place, prepared for life, master of fortune and misfortune ... the soul, buoyant, indestructible, sailing space for-

ever, visiting every region, as a ship the sea."

The glimpse of an Instruction Book previously known "only to God"[2] came through the pursuit of ideas, ideas of the unknown and of unreality.[3] The restless soul "buoyant, indestructible, sailing space forever, visiting every region, as a ship the sea" is the essence of the Human Being. "Has the body a soul? No. The soul has a body."[5]

I have supposed a Human Being to be capable of various physical states, and varying degrees of consciousness, as follows: '(a) the ordinary state, with no consciousness of the presence of Fairies; '(b) the 'eerie' state, in which, while unconscious of actual surroundings, he is also conscious of the presence of Fairies; '(c) a form of trance, in which, while unconscious of actual surroundings, and apparently asleep, he (i.e., his immaterial essence) migrates to other scenes, in the actual world, or in Fairyland, and is conscious of the presence of Fairies.

– *Lewis Carroll*
Preface to *Sylvia and Bruno,* 1857

CHAPTER THREE

THROUGH THE LOOKING GLASS

"WHO IN THE WORLD AM I? AH, THAT'S the great puzzle," wrote Lewis Carroll and, like Alice, we must go through the Looking Glass to find out who we really are. We are more than we seem to be on the surface. We underestimate ourselves when we take ourselves "at face value."

Through the Looking Glass? How do we go through a looking glass? Do we have to go through a mirror to find out who we really are? Figuratively speaking, yes, we have to go beyond the reflection, see below the surface — not like an x-ray, more like insight — if we wish to find out who we really are. It is not a simple thing to do, but it is rewarding if you try.

Let's try now, and for a short time in the privacy of the next few pages let your thoughts move about freely in the weightlessness of your mind. Let go of your surface self, and go beyond the reflection that you see in the mirror; let's try to go through the looking glass and get acquainted with our whole self, the real me.

Letting go is the difficult part, but there are ways to make it easier, not shortcuts, but aids. One aid is of Eastern origin — meditation — which helps us to set our mind free of our bodily frame. This passive way is also restful, and promotes bodily health. Another aid is of Western origin — visualization — which seeks to fill our mind with goals to be achieved rather than to empty it into nothingness. This active way is filled with mental images that we hold up before us as beacons to guide our course. "I have a dream" was the rallying cry of Martin Luther King, Jr., around which an emerging people united to strengthen their cause for Human Rights in the 1960's. Our visualizations help us to see ourselves in context with our situation; to view ourselves objectively; to gain a point of leverage over our present condition; to move obstacles, and to move ourselves along. The Eastern way and the Western way both help us to go through the reflective screen over life, and there is no reason to limit our choice to the one or to the other. I find both helpful, but if I had to choose, I would choose visualization. With mental images, we can simulate; we can foresee and forecast; we can reach out and set goals, we can move along. For me, rest and restfulness are preparations for new endeavors, not goals in themselves.

OUR BASIC COMPONENTS

Much has been written about the way to meditation: proper breathing, yoga, alpha, and nirvana. Medical science contains records of practitioners whose bodily frames defied the laws of medicine while under the spell of deep meditation. They certainly went through the reflective screen of life.

But not enough has been written about the way of visualization — of biofeedback, willpower, initiative, creativity — yet our Western world has been built upon the mental images which individuals visualized, and then in groups materialized. It has been through visualization that we have moved along while other parts of the world slept on. It is with visualizations that the emergent nations pattern themselves on us. What is this aid? What are the components we have to use, and how do we use them?

Music has its notes, its score. Art has its colors, its canvas. Science has its elements, its formula. Each activity has its method of assembling its basic components into a complex and useful whole. Moreover, once a level of proficiency is achieved, by an individual in assembling the components, a new element is introduced, namely improvisation, and we then begin to improvise to suit our individual taste. Our creative moods and talents combine to give vibrance — to bring to life — the objects of our attention. We have gone below the surface, beyond the reflection, through the looking glass when we became familiar with the works of a great composer, a great artist, a great scientist. But when the object is our self, what then? How do we become familiar with our basic components? How do we come to know our self?

THE STARS AT NIGHT

It will help to digress a moment before going further, in order to set a context for the question and, more importantly, for the answer. Just as the sun obstructs our view of the starry sky, and it is only after the sun goes down that we can see the stars. In a similar way, we cannot see our whole self until we turn down the brilliance of our physical presence, and let our mind have access to our metaphysical side as well. We are mesmerized by our physical reflection in the mirror, and we must break this surface tension before we can go below the surface and explore what's there.

The context of the question is to question the basic components: their sovereignty, their usefulness, their hold over us. We tend to accept them without question, and to relate ourselves to the sum of our parts. But that is the physical presence we must tone down if we are to journey through the looking glass. It is in that context that we now take inventory of our basic components and question their sovereignty over us, not to belittle any one of them, but to tone down their collective brilliance so that we may see our stars and know what our whole, complex and useful self includes, so that we may visualize our destiny, and move toward it.

TAKING INVENTORY

Quietly now, and slowly, let us begin to tone down the brilliance of our physical surroundings. Here is where an understanding of meditation will aid us. Take on an alpha image; we want the heavens to beckon us;

we want the stars to shine through. Let your brain idle, and let your mind roam free. Begin to look around in the twilight of your mind. Start with familiar objects, and let's take an inventory of them in a new context, in a new light.

BASIC COMPONENTS	THEIR USEFULNESS
Our eyes:	Do our eyes see, or do we see through our eyes? *Who is the seer?*
Our ears:	Do our ears hear, or do we hear through our ears? *Who is the hearer?*
Our voice:	Does our voice speak, or do we speak through our voice box? *Who is the speaker?*
Our fingers:	Do our fingers feel, or do we feel with our fingers? *Who is the feeler?*
Our brain:	Does our brain think, or do we think with our brain? *Who is the thinker?*

Who is the seer, hearer, speaker, feeler, thinker? Where does this sovereignty lie, in each separate part, or with me? What force within me is more than the sum of my parts? What force within me directs these component parts? Who is seeing through my eyes, speaking through my voice box, judging what is seen and heard? Who in the world am I? Who is the real me?

The answers to these questions lie just ahead, but first it is necessary to continue to question. The answers themselves are not as important as the act of questioning. The willingness to question, the initiative and thought in questioning are important, for the beginning of all wisdom is to question, to ask the right question. If we accept that our eyes see, and our brain thinks, we give sovereignty to them. If we see our self in the context with our parts (see both with our eyes and through them) then we establish sovereignty over our component parts, and increase their utility in our whole self. A blind person knows this better than a person with full sight, for a blind person "sees" through senses other than eyes, and gains insight. Certain handicaps sharpen other senses and serve to build our inner resources. To this extent, we may strive to see through our eyes, and judge not what the eyes see, but what we see, of what we know out of our whole life experience. Therein lie the varying degrees of physical brilliance which we must be adept at toning down in order to be able to work with visualization and to see beyond the reflective surface of our lives.

KNOW THYSELF, FIRST

I have been leading up to defining Human Being, but before advancing a definition I felt it necessary to look at ourselves in context with our complex whole, more than just the sum of our physical parts. Alice put it in terms of a great puzzle. The Talmud put it into these words, "Examine the contents, not the bottle." Solon gave us the injunction, "Know thyself, first." The object was the same for all — to go through the looking glass.

Holding up our basic components for questioning is a first step in the journey. To open a passage to the inner force that motivates us, we must learn how to form mental images of that passageway and our movement through it.

OUR COMPLEX SELF

If you ask me who I am, I answer most readily to my first name. My last name is family, but my first name is me. Is that a clue? If I have an inner force, what is the name for it? Is the name for my inner force my name? Is that me? Am I the energy that activates my components? Am I the incandescence that shines through a smile? Or am I known by some other name? How do I visualize myself? What is a self-image? It may help us find the answer through indirection, and start by answering what a self-image is not.

A self-image is not the reflective surface-image, not just the physical container. Can we agree on that? Nor is a self-image a detached attitude, suspended in time and space from our worldly lives. A self-image is neither container alone nor contents uncontained.

Our visualization of a self-image is more complex than this. Our visualization of a self-image brings contents and container together, one interacting with the other. But how do we visualize such a relationship? The relationship between contents and container is the key, for when we visualize the correct relationship between our physical self and our spiritual self we shall see our whole self; we shall have the correct self-image, and then we can construct a definition for ourselves, for Human Beings.

FINDING OUR SELF

How do we come to know our self? How do we find our self? Let's try some visualizations of containers with contents until we find one that most nearly fits us.

Thinking calls for images, and images contain thought. Think of a bottle of wine; try to visualize it, not to drink from it yet. Is the mental picture of a bottle of wine helpful, an aid to knowing our self? No, I think not, for there is no interaction between the bottle and the wine. The contents do not work with the container; the wine is oblivious to the bottle.

Let's then try another image: a loaf of bread.

Does the visualization of a loaf of bread help us to know our self? No, I think not, for the end product, bread, is only matter. It is true that the yeast does interact with the dough to make the bread, but there is no active energy remaining in the bread to move the mass. We are more than mass, more than matter.

What combination has both mass and energy? Shall we try to visualize an automobile battery, or a flashlight? Does the mental picture of a power cell help us to know our self? No, I think not, but we have come closer for there is an interaction between the contents and the container, which produces energy and light; there is an active energy running through the mass. However, it falls short of our requirement because it must be operated by a third party, and that is intolerable to us. We have an inner force, which will not tolerate third-party sovereignty. Self-determination and free will are more important to us than life itself. A flashlight is not a self-image for us.

Like what then? What is the self-image that more correctly suits us? How do we visualize our multidimensional self? How do we conceptualize our physical mass and our metaphysical energy interacting, and from this fusion extract the essence of conscience, creativity, soul, spirit, and other unique characteristics of self?

Is the key word fusion? Fusion is a complex focus of mass and energy interacting. Fusion is an interaction, that sustains a chain reaction, an interaction that requires no third party to operate. That is more correctly what our self-image wants to be, a visualization most akin to us.

How do we see our self in context with fusion? How do we view our self in a relationship of mass and energy interacting to sustain our actions? How do we relate our self to the process of fusion if we visualize our source of energy (an endless source of energy) interacting with our source of mass (a limited source of mass)? Can it work? It is unlike other forms of fusion with which we are familiar because it is multidimensional. But it does work. The challenge is to understand how it works, which is the challenge posed by every new thing. We have something new to deal with here. Let's try to visualize it.

DARKNESS AND LIGHT

Our form of fusion is not like the sun. There is no darkness on the sun, only light. Darkness has no substance of its own; it is solely the absence of light. Yet we know darkness, just as we seek enlightenment. Our darkness, however, is evidence of a need to build an energy level sufficient to see our self in our own light. When light dims and shadows fall over life, we have a sign to check-up on the ratio of our energy to our mass. Darkness comes from loss of light. Try to visualize an inner light which gives incandescence to your mass, an inner light that you find attractive in others, and which attracts others to you. Take pains to sustain your inner light and there will be little or no darkness in your life. Visualize a self-regulating fusion of mass and energy, and assume responsibility for its proper performance.

This questioning has now brought us to the concept of self-regulating fusion of the physical and the spiritual. With this self-image we are free to improvise to suit our creative moods and talents, and construct a multitude of thought-pictures. Who do we think we are? Who do we want to be?

Of these two questions, the last should be first, because *we become as we think* and therefore we should first decide who we want to be, and *then* we should think about who we are.

This concept of self-constructability is not unlike the concept of self-fulfilling prophecy, only it suggests a more active role for us. We take part, an active part in who we become. This in turn puts a premium on our creative thought process.

We are creative. We create. We create new forms of material, and we create new forms of living systems. More importantly, we act upon ourselves; we become as we think. Just as simple evolution gave way to emergent evolution in our complex selves, we have emerged as a self-regulating fusion of mass and of energy — a greater whole, a new thing.

We are the only contents which sets itself the task of redesigning its container. This emergent property of self-constructability in the wrong hands can be as evil as National Socialism under Hitler was in recent history. We are inherently revolutionary, and must constantly be on guard against arrogant pride, which the Greeks knew was Mankind's besetting sin.

WHO DO WE WANT TO BE?

Like a surveyor who needs a reference point to maintain a direction to know where the balance point lies, we seek a reference point to maintain the direction of our thoughts, to know who we are and where we are heading. There are penalties for using a wrong reference point; a building may collapse or a ship may capsize if we fail to find the balance point. In our own lives, we have enough examples of the penalties exacted from the use of wrong reference points to convince us of that. It is a given that one of the underlying flaws in our thinking that led us to wage war upon one another is our dedication to conflicting ideologies. We may have led ourselves into these conflicts by an imbalance in our container/contents self-imagery. If so, wars arising out of differences in ideologies could be better resolved by changing our self-image than by any peace-making apparatus yet devised.

Since a consequence of our complex-self is that we become as we think, it is obvious that who we think we are is vital to us. For example, if we think we are serfs, beholden to masters, we behave like serfs. When we change that self-image and think of ourselves as free individuals, with self-determination, we become free.

Who do we want to be? What is a right direction for our thoughts? What is a reference point that will guide us to a balance point upon which we can construct a building which will not collapse, a ship that will not capsize?

Since 1859, the reference point that guides us even to today is based upon Darwin's *Origins of Species*. Our attention has been focused on the search for fossils in the graveyard of bones. However, our focus should not be on **where did we come from?** but **where are we bound?** We have visualized ourselves in the image that Desmond

Morris labeled us in *The Naked Ape*.[6] Is this the right direction for our thoughts? Is this who we want to be?

As a teenager during the Great Depression and as a warrior during World War II, I learned to focus on the forest, not the trees. I thought more in terms of destination and how to get there. Darwin, to me, became an obstacle to overcome, and I began to read, make notes, and eventually arranged to meet Desmond Morris in my personal pursuit of the nagging image of the "naked ape".

Desmond Morris is the foremost anthropologist of present-day focus on the origins of the species. Going one-on-one with him was an opportunity not to be missed. It happened in a favorable setting — an art gallery. In addition to his many books, Morris is also an artist who once shared his studio with Miro. His oil paintings gained a wide audience in England, and were brought to New York City by my wife's invitation to Shippee Gallery. Over the course of a week together, we debated the pros and cons of Darwinism, of origins and of destination, but I remained unpersuaded with the present state of affairs that prevailed in our cultural ties to mammelian descent. The maze of contradictory theories finally drove me back to the "origins" of the writings themselves and I immersed myself in the correspondence and publications of Darwin and his collaborator, Wallace. There, stripped of the sensational headlines and distortions of a hungry press, a different picture began to emerge. My findings were far different from the popular images of Darwinism and like a reliable reference point to guide us as we lay our ground work for a viable future.

In the next chapter, *Darwin Revisited,* join me as we guide our thoughts through the maze to a reliable reference point. Give Darwin his due and special place in the evolution of botany. Give Wallace his due for foreseeing a then unforeseeable future for mankind. Recognize the role of emergent evolution that points to Wallace's prediction: We become as we think.

Man, with all his noble qualities, with sympathy which feels for the most debased, with benevolence which extends not only to other men but to the humblest living creature, with his god-like intellect which has penetrated into the movements and constitution of the solar system — with all these exalted powers — Man still bears in his bodily frame the indelible stamp of his lowly origin."

– *Charles Darwin*
The Descent of Man

DARWIN REVISITED: WEB OF CHANGE

D ARWIN RECOGNIZED THAT THE PROGENY of a species may be a new species and through the use of his phrase "god-like intellect" accepted mankind as a new thing. There is no question that Darwin also viewed man as part of the web of evolutionary change; the question is why did he focus solely on the bodily frame and ignore the god-like intellect? The answer lies in his fascination with botany. He addressed man through nature, not man in his uniqueness.

Darwin had an original thought in the concept of physical evolution through natural selection, but he left it incomplete; he did not permit the idea itself to evolve. Evolution is a process ranging from the simple to the complex, with changes in character at different stages. It is axiomatic that various types of animals and plants have their origin in other pre-existing types. In his *Origin of Species*,[7] Darwin advanced this theory applying to all of Nature, except Mankind. Whether out of peer pressure or fear of the religious persecution rampant at the time, his theory of evolution, circa 1859, was applied only to plant and animal life, not to man. It was to be twelve years later that Darwin published *The Descent of Man*[8] from which the opening quotation for this chapter is drawn. Although Darwin holds fast to his "tree-of-life" imagery when he concludes that "Man still bears in his bodily frame the indelible stamp of his lowly origin," it should not be overlooked that he first proclaimed, "Man, with his god-like intellect which has penetrated into the movements and constitution of the solar system ...".

Darwin possessed a towering intellect. He studied himself as a Being of intellect as well as a Being in nature. He turned to himself for creative thought, and for the authority which flows from it. He knew that he knew. He was a Knower. But his subject was plant and animal life, not Mankind.

CONTENTS AND CONTAINER

There are many ways of saying the same thing, and Darwin's way of saying container was "bodily frame." At the same time he spoke of "God-like intellect" as we might speak of contents.

In an earlier century, the Talmud spoke of the container and its contents in a different way: "Examine the contents, not the bottle." And earlier still, Solon gave us the injunction "Know thyself, first."

From earlier times, individuals have known of their origins and have pointed to the heavens and still do. The real question, which has been raised by Darwinism, a question which has unnecessarily become a source of conflict between religion and science is this: Which origins are we referring to, thoseof our contents or those of our container?

Obviously, the Talmud referred to the contents, and was explicit in rejecting the container: "…not the bottle." Solon was more Delphic: "Know thyself, first," But there can be no doubt as to the nature of *thyself* in his imagery. Neither is there room for doubt in Darwin's theory: It was directed toward the container, not the contents.

Darwin was a working scientist, a geologist and a botanist. His focus was on the bottle. But he was not alone in 1859 when he published his first work on Natural Selection. Independently, and in the same year, Alfred Russell Wallace published his first work on the same subject but with a different conclusion. Wallace focused upon our uniqueness in nature, and concluded that our contents had a new and different origin, anticipating the theory of emergent evolution with the proposition that our spirit "must have another origin."

Once the distinction was made, the two paths parted, and Darwin later wrote Wallace, confirming their separate paths. "I have collected a few notes on man, but I do not suppose that I shall ever use them … Do you intend to follow out your views, and if so, would you like at some future time to have my few references and notes?" Wallace did, and he went on to publish a paper discussing the limits of the principle of natural selection as applied to man. He argued that the principle had applied to man's precursors, but that man, after attaining a high degree of intellect, no longer remained subject to the rule of natural selection. He concluded that man's highly developed moral and intellectual facilities had not resulted from the operation of natural law. Twenty-five years later, Wallace published his definitive work under the title "Darwinism: An Exposition of the Theory of Natural Selection," in which he held that "man's body may have been developed from that of a lower animal form under the law of natural selection, but man now possesses intellectual and moral faculties which have another origin in the unseen universe of the Spirit." Wallace began to focus on "contents," to differentiate the contents from the container.

THE TANGLED WEB

Although Darwin did foresee a "far more perfect creature in the making," over the years his views have been distorted and his name has come to personalize the conflict which has clouded our thoughts about evolution for the past 150 years, and continues today to intrude upon our educational system, even into our newspaper supplements and our daily life. On July 8, 1980, *The New York Times* Science Section's lead story was, "Surprising Similarity Found in Humans and Apes," by Howard M. Schmeck, Jr. On February 7, 1980, it was, "Monkey-like African Primate Called Common Ancestor of Man and Apes," by Bogard Webster. On October 21, 1979, it was, "Scientists At Odds on Receptivity of Primates to Human Language," by Davis Sobel, and in the same issue a new book by

Adrian J. Desmond, *The Apes' Reflection: Are We About to Suffer A New Identity Crisis?* was reviewed. There seems to be no end to our fascination with our animal ancestry; worse still, we seem to relish it.

Darwin thought of evolution as a web of change, but his thesis became tangled in our minds and we became caught in the tangled web. The more we struggle, the tighter it gets, and it pulls us down as we strain against it. It would be amusing if it were not serious. But because it is serious, we should do something about it. What to do and how to go about it are the questions we now face.

What to do, it seems to me, is to regain our perspective, and *How to go about it* is to take the advice of the Talmud, "Examine the contents". We should try to identify the key elements of our contents, and then define them until they gradually become well known to us, no longer as a tangled web but as a clear line of thought.

HOMO SAPIENS VS HUMAN BEINGS

How do we clear a muddy stream? We go back to the source. How do we clear our line of thought? We should do the same thing, go back to the source.

The emergence of Homo sapiens is correlated with a cultural change that took place approximately 35,000 years ago, in proof of which we have concrete evidence in the form of cave art.

The emergence of Human Beings, on the other hand, is correlated with other, different cultural changes that took place only within the past 3,500 years, including the abstract aspects of philosophy and poetry and religion.

Perhaps it would be sapient to define Homo sapiens first and by comparison highlight the definition of the new word Human Beings. From *Webster's Seventh New Collegiate Dictionary* we learn that Homo sapiens is a species name meaning, "wise animal", as distinguished from fossil man. Homo sapiens is modern man.

In a more explicit definition of Homo sapiens, Byron Kurten in 1970 wrote in *Not From The Apes* that:

> "Homo sapiens is easily distinguished from typical Neanderthal men. The eyebrow ridges of the former are weak or absent, the forehead is steeper, the back of the head more rounded, the eye sockets angular, the face less protruding, the teeth smaller, and the chin more prominent. The brain cage is on the average somewhat smaller than in the Neanderthal, but it varies in extreme cases from about 1000 cc to twice that volume. The skull bones are thinner, and the face more delicate than the Neanderthals. The limp bones, too, are more delicate and the chest flatter and less barrel-like. Many other anatomical details could be added."

Here, certainly is a simple definition of Homo sapiens the container. It presents us with the temptation to construct an equally simple definition of Human Beings as the contents. But this is a temptation to be avoided, because we are not simply dealing with separate parts. We are dealing with different entities. The difference between these entities can be seen in the simplicity of the one as opposed to the complexity of the other.

Human is akin to homo but it relates more to characteristics than to similarities.

Human is closely related to humane, a trait which is marked by compassion, sympathy, and consideration of other forms of life. Human, therefore, is as different from homo as the complex is different from the simple.

Being, likewise, means more than simple existence. Being is Spirit. Everything else is in a state of becoming. "God is in a state of Being" is the definition Robertson gave in 1853. No more apt name nor better words could describe us than Human Beings. How far we have fallen short of our potential and how far we have yet to grow will never be judged until we construct a definition of ourselves that stands for the potential that we have within and the reality that we become.

Before we undertake the work on the structure of words, one last word on Darwin. No comment herein is meant to minimize him in any way as a creative Human Being who employed his life usefully in advancing the frontiers of our thoughts. It is not with Darwin that issue is taken; it is with the misuse of Darwin's thoughts by others.

DEFINITION OF WORDS

How to regain our perspective? Let us begin with a fresh definition of words, to understand better what Darwin and Wallace were writing about.

The words they used were ordinary words, but those same words have taken on extraordinary meanings since the time they so innocently used them. We need to return to their times and try to understand the innocent use of their key words. They are as follows:

EVOLUTION: a theory that various types of animals and plants have their origin in other pre-existing types and that distinguishing differences are due to modifications in successive generations by natural selection.

CONTINUITY: the uninterrupted connection or union with pre-existing types.

TREE (GENEALOGICAL): a diagram that depicts a branching from an original stem.

CONCENTRIC: having a common center, but unconnected to it.

CIRCLE: an area of action or influence; a group bound by a common tie.

EMERGENT EVOLUTION: evolution characterized by the appearance at different levels of wholly new and unpredictable characteristics or qualities through a rearrangement of pre-existent entities.

In the foregoing list, if the last definition were to be examined first we would have less difficulty with what follows. For convenience then, let's start with:

EMERGENT EVOLUTION: a process which is open-ended, and which proceeds from the simple to the complex until the process reaches the highest point of complexity of interacting parts and fusion takes place, thereby developing a new entity. Thus begins anew the process of evolution of the new entity as a new thing. At the stage of complexity of cross-connections where fusion takes place, acceleration is achieved and we find that versatility increases rapidly with complexity. At this level, natural selection is no longer a controlling force within the process of evolution. Rather, intellectual adaptability becomes the controlling force and self-constructibility becomes one of the complex stages of emergent evolution.

Wallace called it a self-acting process. It was his conviction that the rise of organic life, the rise of consciousness, and the rise of man represent jumps in the evolutionary process. With emergent in mind as a modifier to evolution, we can separate out the questions of natural selection and of genealogical tree without much difficulty. But what of the theory of continuity and its persistent search for the missing link?

The real troublemaker among our defined words is *continuity*. Continuity unfortunately contains the notion of uninterrupted connection that we must be rid of, for it tangles our thoughts and leads us up blind alleys and into dead ends in search for "the missing link." This meaning of "continuity' is a Darwinian knot that we must untie before we can be free to think clearly, because it is in the center of the tangled web.

Tree (genealogical), with its trunk and all its branches, can stay in our thoughts, not as a lone tree but rather as a forest of many and varied trees. Trees may themselves be branches of a botanical tree, but that does not make man a branch of an animal tree.

Concentric and **circle** will give us no trouble. These words help to open our minds to think more clearly about what the meaning of evolution really is — a process from the simple to the complex. It is a process that encourages growth, and permits functions to give rise to new functions. Darwin focused upon natural selection and became mesmerized with it as a static thing rather than as a stage in a continuing process. Wallace forged ahead; his thinking was in harmony with the process of evolution, a process from the simple to the complex.

OUR LIVING SYSTEMS

Our unique development is the product of the inter-action of our parts. Development per se is not an unfold-ing of parts already assembled; it is a new thing. Variation and selection are subject to natural selection only up to the point that intellect begins to be employed. Individual variations are then creatively adapted. Once this viewpoint is gained, we see more clearly the thread of thought that resolved the differences between science and religion in Wallace's mind. Unfortunately this con-cept is not wide spread today.

How to give equal time to the proposition that we hold something unique within us, something that must be reckoned with and brought into harmony and bal-ance with the whole of us? Would worthwhile results greet us if we clear our thoughts and are able to see beyond the stresses and the conflicts of the tangled web of Darwinian evolution? What would we see? We should see ourselves not as a reflection of the ape. We should see ourselves in the light of our own incandescence, a new thing. We should see ourselves not as a wise animal, but as a Human Being. Then we would begin to think. We would begin to interact intelligently with our new thoughts, and to grow with them. Our development is no longer subject to natural selection. Our development is rather an intellectual interaction, the result of the fusion of our mind and our body. We become as we think. As we redirect our minds from thinking of our-selves as human animals toward thinking of ourselves as Human Beings, we release our minds from the biological pull of animal traits, and begin to act more like Human

Beings, which is to say qualified beings with a destiny to come into Being. We become as we think, and as we materialize that which we think, so we begin to materialize Being. From this beginning, there is only a short step remaining to the immortality of Being, and that short step is within our reach.

When we see beyond the tangle, and see ourselves as Human Beings; we have a duty to pause in order not to repeat the error, which resulted in the controversy 150 years ago. We have a duty to define our words carefully so that everyone can see clearly the line of thought ahead and follow it, maintaining equilibrium, balance, and harmony, avoiding unnecessary tangles and pitfalls along the way.

The Human Being

Human Being: ('hyu-men be-in) n. 1. a Being with human attributes; 2. the image of God cast into human form; 3. a genus of recent times (B.C./A.D.) identified with creative thought, capable of materializing concepts, associated with structured thought and creative powers; 4. a new breed with a superior force, the force not only to unlock nature's safe and to open up the secret files, but also to become one with nature and participate in the process called life as a vessel of Being, each with its own ethereal contents; to participate not as a guardian but as a gardener, entrusted with the presence of Being; v. 1. the coming into Being of a human, the filling of a human vessel with Being; 2. the fusion of human nature with ethereal nature, the interaction of the physical with the ethereal, resulting in the formulation of a new force, the incandescent self, the Human Being.

CHAPTER FIVE

THE HUMAN BEING: ONE GIANT LEAP

L IFE IS A PROCESS OF BECOMING, A sequence of states we go through. It reverses when we select a state and choose to remain in it, or are unable to rise above it because of some restraint imposed upon us. The resultant stagnation becomes a blight upon life.

The 20th Century has had its share of the states we go through when some restraint is imposed upon us, as was the example in Europe before World War II in Communist Russia. But there are even more frightful examples of the blight upon life in the half century following the War.

The restraints imposed by Russia during the cold war were felt in Poland, Romania, and other nations under Russian control, but there was no more vivid example than in East Germany, where events slowed down to a standstill and stagnation brought blight upon life in general. The contrast was made more real as West Germany grew and prospered under the freedom granted by the North Atlantic Treaty Organization. The Berlin

Wall became the focal point and symbol of this schism in Germany, and when it fell following the end of communism in Russia, it finally exposed for the world to see just how appalling the situation had become when the restraints imposed upon a people imprisoned them.

Although the fall of communism in Europe renewed the process of becoming in Europe, other adverse conditions continued around the world, in North Korea, for example, with its contrasting example in South Korea, and in China, where the huge land mass obscured the extent of the situation.

In lesser but also meaningful examples, economical stagnation nearer to home in South America began to get notice as democracy came to focus upon itself. The benefits of free trade in North America with Canada, Mexico and the United States were offered to the countries of South America in a hemisphere meeting in Quebec in April, 2001, but limited to those with democratic governments.

Political concepts are not the only source that may threaten stagnation and stunt personal growth. As wonderful as science is, it also threatens stagnation because it limits us to grow beyond the elements of proof. It limits the definition of knowledge to include our innate capability of knowing dimensions other than the physical. We would be becoming, rather than stagnating, if we extended our definition of knowledge to include the unknowables as well as the knowables and allow ourselves to grow beyond the limitations of proof.

Becoming in itself is the process of life. Rising above what we have been requires a new concept, the concept of a living system with the continuity of motion. The concept that "we become as we think" give leverage to the increase of self-esteem.

If, indeed, we become as we think, much will change once we begin to think of ourselves as Human Beings. As we begin to search for links to Being rather than for links to fossils, we shall raise our self-awareness and improve our self-esteem, our confidence in our own merit as individuals. Then we will have a common concept of who we are, a unifying concept. No longer do we need to stumble in our speech over the choice of him or her, black or white, or among Jew, Christian, or Buddhist. The collective noun Human Being will do. As Neil Armstrong said when he stepped down to the moon's surface, "That's one small step for a man — one giant leap for Mankind."

EVEN A SLIGHT CHANGE

What would a slight change in our self-esteem do to our attitudes toward everything we do? Even a slight change at the source will change everything that flows therefrom. A rise in a few degrees at the pole would increase the volume of the oceans and change the shape of the continents.

Who do we think we are? What are we becoming? What could we change by changing our thoughts? Archimedes said, "Give me a place to stand on and I can move the earth." Tolstoy said, "The progress of humanity arising from a multitude of individual wills would reflect itself in one's own merit as an individual, and the level of self-esteem would increase the volume of good-will and change the shape of human relationships around the world."

What is a Human Being? What are Human Beings? They don't come in ideologies, nor do they come in any color, or particular shape or size. If you think you have seen one you are probably mistaken, because a camera cannot reproduce one, nor an artist render one's likeness. The nearest you can get is to catch the glint through an eye, or the toss of the head, but reflectively you cannot present one. You can, however, know one and become one.

What is our visualization of a Human Being? A Human Being is more than matter, and that matters. If we are simply matter, we could know nothing at all, for there is nothing so inconceivable as to say that matter knows itself. A Human Being is a Knower, one who knows, and knows that he knows; he knows the knowable and unknowable. Knowledge in this sense is a separate subject that follows in Chapter VI but is relevant to the construction of a definition of Human Being.

There is more to us than we know, and we must provide room in our definition for that which we cannot know. Knowables are subject to proof; unknowables are open to experience. A Human Being has the capability of dealing with both and of drawing upon one for the other. What then is the definition of a Human Being? What is our reference point?

THE CASE FOR UPPER CASE

The dictionary is our reference point, the point where definitions are held in safe keeping. Lower and upper case is a vital distinction in a definition, a distinction I became aware of only as I began research for this second volume of the trilogy: *Becoming — The Human Being — Being*. Lower case human is a defined word and lower case being is a defined word, but there is no defined word *Human Being*. None, anywhere. Neither does the plural *Human Beings* exist as a defined word in our language, ancient or modern. Soul yes, in many forms, but not as a fusion of both the body and the soul that distinguishes the Human Being. I have no explanation for Human Beings' absence as a proper noun, but there is a simple solution to the problem: Fill the void by constructing the word.

Since it is ourselves we are defining, let us give our definition the status of upper case: Human Being. And since we are not a replacement for Homo sapiens , but rather a whole new word, let us carefully construct a definition to reflect our status as a new thing.

THE NEW WORD

How shall we define Human Beings as a noun and verb, and then convey the meaning of this complex development? Not just the distinction between a container and its contents, but the distinction between a simple container and a container with contents in the act of fusion which creates a new thing? It will not be easy to structure a definition for Human Beings, but that is all the more reason to start now.

The concept for our new word is not related to evolution. Here the concept is concerned with a characteristic of our complex self, an emerging property of ourselves, our self-constructability. To herald it, I have chosen the phrase, "We become as we think".

Like a broad and deep chasm, separating us from ourselves, Darwinism obstructs our free consideration of this concept of self-constructability. The misapplication of Darwinism is the probable cause for the persistent use of Homo sapiens as the species name for Mankind. It is also the probable cause for the absence of Human Being from our dictionaries. The misapplication of Darwinism is the reason why I felt obliged to go back and take a fresh look at Darwin, to try to read into the context of his time and place the limited meaning of his words. Until we have freed our thoughts from the misapplication of Darwinism, we shall continue to suffer the limitations of containerism.

Are not these limitations one of the major sources of flaws in our troubled society? Since we are a complex structure of mind and matter, and since we are self-constructing in our intellectual adaptability to the living systems, it matters greatly who we think we are, and so long as we think of ourselves as Homo sapiens, we tend to become animal-like, like super animals.

What would change if we changed our word for Mankind from Homo sapiens to Human Beings? It is time to find out. But first, we must construct a suitable definition for Human Beings and so clear our thoughts, for we do become as we think.

HUMAN BEING DEFINED

The definition of Human Being is difficult enough in the abstract but is impossible in the concrete, except to say what it is not. A Human Being is the opposite of simple; a Human Being is complex and multidimensional. A Human Being is not a single structure, and its multidimensional structure does not function independently from nor obliviously to its various elements. A Human Being is not a spectator in a creative universe, but rather a participant. A Human Being is creative, is a creator of new forms of life as well as new forms of materials.

More importantly, Human Beings act creatively upon themselves, for we become as we think. Human Beings are a new breed with superior force. This is the force not only to unlock nature's safe and to open up the secret files, but also to become one with nature, and to participate in the process called life as a vessel of Being, a qualified Being, a Human Being.

There is something concrete in Chapter VI, several Schematic Diagrams on Knowledge that may help us with our definition of Human Being. It is a series of diagrams that separate the knowables and the unknowables, and give sub-divisions with characteristics for each. On the left side, the heading is *Human*, and on the right side the heading is *Being*. *Human* and *Being* — the interaction of matter and energy, the fusion of the physical with the spiritual, the emergent property of self-constructability in a complex system of life, the self image that Alice in Wonderland sought. The real me.

Who in the world am I? The answer is that we become as we think. Can we relate our present misfortunes to our past self-images? Who have we thought we were? Who do we think we are? Let us construct a definition and see.

CONSTRUCTING A DEFINITION OF HUMAN BEING

As a noun:
— a Being with human attributes
— the image of God cast into human form
— vessel of Being, with its own ethereal contents
— a gardener entrusted with the cultivation of Being

As a word:
Human Being: ('hyu-men be-in) *n.* **1.** a Being with human attributes; **2.** the image of God cast into human form; **3.** a genus of recent times (B.C./A.D.) identified with creative thought, capable of materializing concepts, associated with structured thought and creative powers; **4.** a new breed with a superior force. This is the force not only to unlock nature's safe and to open up the secret files, but also to become one with nature and participate in the process called life as a vessel of Being, each with its own ethereal contents, to participate not as a guardian but as a gardener, entrusted with the presence of Being; *v.* **1.** the coming into Being of a human, the filling of a human vessel with Being; **2.** the fusion of

human nature with ethereal nature, the interaction of the physical with the ethereal, resulting in the formulation of a new force, the incandescent self, the Human Being.

WE BECOME AS WE THINK

We should give thought to how we think of ourselves. Living up to what is expected of us begins with a clear focus on our self-image. Try copying this definition of Human Being, and in the process of using your own hand to write it out, be creative. Improve on it.

Participate: Take an affirmative action; become part of the solution, for we do become as we think. As we come to understand how our thoughts work upon us, we should reach out to help others become aware of these changes in the air, which flow from the self-image of who we think we are, of who we want to be.

EVEN A SLIGHT CHANGE

What would a slight change in our self-esteem do to our attitude toward everything that we do? Even a slight change at the source will change every thing that flows therefrom. A rise of a few degrees at the pole would increase the volume of the oceans and change the shape of the continents.

Would the distinction between Human Beings and Homo sapiens bring a change in our self-esteem and our attitude toward everything we do? What changed when we saw Neil Armstrong step onto the surface of the moon? In his words, "That's one small step for man … one giant leap for Mankind."

CHAPTER SIX

A BODY OF KNOWLEDGE

IMPORTANT THOUGH IT MAY BE, KNOWLEDGE of our body is a limited objective. Our body of knowledge is something else. Knowledge includes a multitude of things. It reaches out to the modalities of truth and falsehood, good and bad, beauty and ugliness, as well as to facts and fiction, the concrete and the abstract, the physical and the ethereal, matter and mind, all that Mankind has experienced, knows and does.

Mystery is also part of knowledge. The unknown carries with it a demand to be known that we find hard to resist. This demand to be known has kept the controversy over Darwinism alive for over 100 years because it has retained the mystery of the missing link. Otherwise, the controversy has added little to our body of knowledge.

But now, finally, the mystery is being dispelled.

We are finding out that there is no missing link. There is no link at all. Therefore, there is no longer any mystery. The end of the hunt for the link as far as science is concerned came abruptly in 1980 during a four-day

Chicago meeting at the Field Museum of Natural History where 150 scientists met to thrash out a variety of new hypotheses that were challenging older ideas. The mystery of the unknown disappeared in the bright light of their findings. "The pattern that we were told to find for the last 120 years does not exist," declared a speaker from the American Museum of Natural History. "There are a few examples, if any — some say none — of one species shading gradually into another." A speaker from Harvard University reiterated the hypothesis that "new species arise not from gradual changes, but in sudden bursts of evolution change dramatically."

It is important to understand the body — everything we can about the body, how it evolved, how it functions, how it should be maintained and made more resistant to an increasingly hostile environment. But a precise knowledge of the body and its evolution should not be the prolonged subject of a controversy created by Darwinism that has reached into our system of education, where it limits the body of knowledge that we ourselves need if we are to continue to grow. Once we allow a false ceiling to be placed upon our thoughts, we stunt our growth. Through the mystery of the missing link — the concept of linkage itself — Darwinism has held our minds hostage to the notion that we are descended from the apes, and has given us the scientific name of Homo sapiens, wise animals. After six generations of such schooling, we have been programmed to think of ourselves as animals, and our materialistic culture today is a valid mirror of these misguided thoughts. But we are not like animals at all. Animals do not despoil nature; they find a den or build a nest, but they do not lay macadam. It is a misnomer to use the word Homo sapiens at all. We are a new and different species, that has appeared in "a sudden burst of evolution," and we are more likely to find that our missing link is to Being, not to biology.

There are some oases of exceptions. Venice is one.

In Venice, without automobiles, life moves at a different pace. They say in Venice that after only a week a visitor there has shed many of the aggressions developed by the automobile and become "more of a Human Being."

What would we be like if we shed the concept of Darwinism, and thought of ourselves as Human Beings? What would life be like in 120 years if the next six generations were freed from an association with the animal traits developed by the exclusive study of Darwinism, freed to study our whole body of knowledge, not held down to a limited area of matter?

It is not difficult to project our mind forward and visualize the basic changes in society flowing from such a change in our thought processes. One obvious change would be the end of hostility, including warfare, because our minds, once freed from the prison of wise-animalism, would not tolerate war, nor the tools of war, any more than society tolerates slavery today, 140 years after the Emancipation Proclamation. Look back 140 years to that significant change in our thought process and examine its consequences, and then look ahead 140 years and you will begin to measure the comparable changes in our society following the emancipation of the mind from its slavery.

How do we shed Darwinism? How do we free our minds of this limitation? The first stage is to provide a choice. As it stands today, there is no choice: the proper name for Mankind is Homo sapiens.

If we say "art," we may think of Florence, Venice, Paris or New York. If we say "music," we may think of the Philharmonic Orchestra in Philadelphia or Boston. What alternative do we have to Homo sapiens? Indeed, is Homo sapiens a proper name for Mankind at all? Let us think on this matter for awhile, for we become as we think, and it does matter.

MATTER

Are we matter? **No, mind.** *What is mind?* **Never matter.**

Darwin dealt with mind as if it were included in matter. Darwinism thus held mind to be a dimension of matter, which is an inconsistency.

Mind is an extra dimension. Mind does not defer to matter. Matter and energy are modalities. Matter cannot exist without energy, for we know that even solid granite has atoms of energy within its mass. But mind and matter are of different realms. When Darwin dealt with matter as if it included mind, he established a misleading conception of mind and matter, which remains one of the most troublesome aspects of his theory. Mind and matter are not a modality. Mind is not subordinate nor equal to matter; mind is intellect. Wallace classified mind as of spiritual origin, and Darwin himself described mind as god-like intellect early in his work.

Brain is matter, but brain is not the mind. Brain is a physical part of the body, and can function with its own level of energy for most life-support needs, including memory and instinct. But when it comes to creative thought and intellect, it is mind at work, not brain. Brain requires energy, but mind requires more than energy. It requires incandescence or light.

Matter and energy come ready-mixed. They cohabitate. One is always found with the other in some degree. But not mind. Mind stands alone and apart from body, which it commands, and with which it does not readily mix.

Mind is like an eagle, and eagles don't flock. They soar on outstretched wings on up-drafts of invisible winds. Minds love music for that reason. Minds also enjoy flights of fantasy and dreams. Mind works and plays, but its work is in one dimension and its play is in another dimension. We need to observe and to include both dimensions in our body of knowledge. It is from "the other dimension" that the mind draws its creative powers and gathers its insight and enlightenment. Mind is extra-dimensional, it is not matter, nor is it coequal with matter. There is no unity between the two. They are of different existence, one ethereal and the other temporal. One above the other. Mind over matter.

MIND OVER MATTER

If we were merely mind and matter, coequal in all aspects, we wouldn't have the problem we have in reconciling our minds to our material lives because our minds wouldn't object, wouldn't goad us, wouldn't cause us to rebel. We wouldn't know, and long for something more. We are above the level of matter because we do know and we know that we know. We are above the level of matter because it is impossible to conceive that matter knows itself, and yet we are knowers — we know. We are something different from, and more than, the peers of matter.

If we were mind and matter, then the scientific name for Mankind, Homo sapiens, might well be appropriate. A wise animal would be a proper name for such an arrangement, but it doesn't work that way. Mind and matter won't blend. Like oil and water, they won't stay mixed. Mind will surface every time, as the history of Mankind repeats over and over again.

If there is a real fault to find with Darwin, it is not with his creative mind, but rather with his one-track, single-minded approach to his subject. Darwin fell short of a unifying system, and we failed to perceive how limited his track was for the amount of traffic it was asked to bear.

Although Darwin did not directly apply his system to Mankind, neither did he sufficiently nor clearly exclude Mankind from it. For example, nowhere in Darwin's notes on biology is there any reference to the observance of Holy Days, or holidays of any sort by any species of the animal kingdom. Nor did Darwin ever suggest that a cow had any concept of Sunday. Darwin did not try to apply his theory of evolution by natural selection to Mankind specifically for good reason, because survival of the fittest was patently incompatible with the mores of the human race. Through medicine and through conscience, both science and religion are dedicated to keeping alive the weak, disabled, the aged and infirm, the sick and needy.

It was Darwin's single-track obsession with classifying matter and seeking related linkage that caused the traffic problem, and yet it was at least our shared fault that we attempted to make his single-track into our mainline system. However, now that we have finally applied our minds to it, we are finding ways to release the congestion, and new means to resolve the problems caused by his concept of descent.

MIND

Mankind has mind, has intellect, has incandescence, has light, is a new something, an emergent species, new to the system. Mankind has more than energy and matter. Mankind has self-determination, willpower, free will, conscience, creative thought and judgment, all of which are exercised by mind over matter. Mankind is not a wise animal, but rather is a qualified Being, a Human Being.

Mind over matter is the unique structure of Mankind: mind as intellect, as light dispelling darkness, as the generator of Being.

Mind over matter is basic to the uniqueness of Mankind, but it is not the whole story. It is more like the foundation upon which may be built many higher stories. To master matter in the time that our species has had is but a blink in the whole of time. We began with the physical matter of our bodies and of our surroundings. We applied our minds to master these elements of our environment. We explored and recorded and repeated until the sheer bulk of facts challenged our ability to store them, and the last of our physical frontiers for exploration disappeared. Finally, our minds materialized the computer and we delegated matter to deal with matter. Our minds had outgrown the challenge of matter and turned to something more challenging, the mind itself. Mind over mind became our new frontier, the end of our adolescence, the mark of our coming of age. At that point we became adults.

MIND OVER MIND

The injunction "Know thyself, first" is an invitation to apply our mind to our mind to discover our real self. The concept of knowing our self may be confusing if we perceive our self as matter. As matter how could we *know* our self?

The word for knowing our self as matter is not *know*, it is *recognize*.

Yes, you can recognize your self in the mirror, and yet you would not know your real self. To know your self is to direct mind to mind, then you come to know your self. Mind over mind is achieved when you tune into the universal mind, as in silent prayer.

Conscience is mind over mind, as is enlightenment. Once you get through the barrier of physical recognition of matter and get involved in knowing, you identify with mind and use it constantly. You become mind; you become master of your matter. Another dimension is added to your time and space, and gives you leverage over them by adding a new force to your life: enthusiasm, something more than added energy. Enthusiasm comes from *en theos*, Greek for "God within."

THE OTHER DIMENSION

In Chapter VIII, the element of the Unknowables is joined to the element of the Knowables as the sum total of Knowledge.

Here we anticipate this multi-dimensional perception of Knowledge, for in our body of knowledge we know facts as well as fancy. We know the known and we work with the unknown, and more than these, we somehow know the unknowable. This seeming contradiction of terms notwithstanding, we know that we know. We are Knowers.

We have minds which span the finite and infinity; minds that carry us back and forth through different dimensions; minds that interface with the physical and the ethereal; minds that command matter; minds that create new forms of life, materialize thoughts, and generate Being.

"... *Dust thou art, to dust returnest was not spoken of the soul.*"[11]

Our poets tell us better than our scientists of our destiny.

Through the cultivation of our god-like intellect, we come into Being, for we are Human Beings. But what is a Human Being?

Open your mind to the part of you that knows, and knows that it knows; it knows that it survives time and space. It is a part of the universe within you, your window on the universe outside, a part of your life not limited by the duration of your lifetime, a part of your immortal life.

Nathan Shippee

CHAPTER SEVEN

THE BIRTH OF THOUGHT

T RY TO IMAGINE BEING WITHOUT THOUGHT. Not merely to stop thinking, or to rest your mind, but to be without the means of thinking, without the power of imagination. Not to be merely conscious, but to be unable to reason.

We were conscious long before we were thoughtful. Conscious, conscience, consciousness all derive from the same root: to know. Think and thought are different. To think is to give entrance of an idea to the mind, to call to mind, to center one's thoughts. Thought is a reasoning power, the power to imagine, the process of thinking.

If you can imagine yourself only as you see yourself reflected in the mirror, a flat surface with nothing going on inside, and see yourself only as your mirror image is reflected to your eyes, without any interior entity knowingly responding, you will begin to understand that something noteworthy happened when thought was born.

Because we are endowed with thought, we tend to take it for granted. We assume that it always was, and like the unaware owner of an article of real value, fail to credit its proper worth. We find it natural to endow others with what we find commonplace and comfortable in ourselves. Shaw thought that anyone could write; he envied the different talents of others. The athlete finds golf an easy game; the mathematician finds no mystery in numbers, and both expect as much from others. It is little wonder then that we associate thought with mankind and do not wonder what the human race was like before thought, or when thinking came to mankind, or how.

Before the birth of thought, the human species was well along the biological path of evolution. When intelligence in the brain exceeded instinct in the genes, nature combined instinct and intelligence and the human race began to organize group efforts, to form simple societies, and to worship. As a worshipper of many gods, any chosen image became a god, not the image of God. Humans were conscious, knew and saw. But they saw with their eyes, not through them. Humans knew but did not know that they knew; asked, but did not reason why. A person was a spectator, a vassal, a number as much as any number in a herd. And then, some began to think.

FROM VASSAL TO VESSEL

From vassal into vessel the human species was dramatically changed through the birth of thought, and not so long ago. In terms of evolution, it happened within our recorded history. In terms of our times, reflect upon our calendar, for the years since Anno Domini have meaning here. This most recent development in the progress of evolution cast the human race in a new and different role, signaling a new and different world inhabited by new and different beings.

Perhaps it is too recent a development to have earned the recognition that it merits. Even Darwin failed to convey its significance, and succeeded only in churning discord when he titled his pioneer work, *The Descent of Man*. More recently, Bronowski came closer but failed to fully focus our attention with his title for a similar work, *The Ascent of Man*. Bronowski did, however, develop the thesis of the uniqueness of mankind in the progress of evolution, and had he added only one letter in the title of his work, and called it *The Nascent of Man*, he would have conveyed that which happened so recently. For it was our coming into being that we must associate with the birth of thought, the nascence of an eternal life process within the biological life process. It is necessary to understand the significance of what happened if we are to appreciate that this event was a change in the very nature of the human race. For when mankind became manned, nature revealed her secrets. Through the power of thought, the unseen atom was visualized, the building blocks of life were translated into chemical formulas, and travel to distant stars became as certain as used to be the nomadic journeys of herdsmen from season to season. But before we examine too deeply the meaning of what happened to our state of being when thought was born, which was fairly recently, it may help us to understand if we know in more detail when it happened, and how it came about.

THE NEW POWER

When did mankind become manned, and how did it come about? It is not presumptuous to ask, for the inquisitive mind of mankind never rests and is capable of more than we credit it. Thought is to the mind what appetite is to the body. To keep asking questions is to keep the mind well fed. Descartes served us an appetizer, but stopped short of a whole meal. Had he followed, "I think; therefore I am" with the question: "I am what?", we would have had more substantial food for thought, and perhaps could have answered him three hundred and fifty years sooner with the remark, "I am to think."

The birth of thought, not just the past tense of thinking, but rather the full powers of reasoning, took place during a thousand-year period about 3,000 years ago. It can be fixed because it was recorded in the literature of the time. Prior to that time, there is no recorded concept of free will; instructions were given from afar, decisions were sought from graven images. People warred because the gods told them it was propitious to do so. The people of those times did not sit down and reason out their next move. They had no wills of their own and certainly no reasoning power. It is difficult for us now to imagine what it was like then. Back then, the gods took the place of individual thought. It was not an invention, like the machine gun or tank, or other technological improvement that gave the victors their victory. It was a transcending evolutionary development which gave the new breed a superior power, the power not only to unlock nature's safe and open up the secret files, but also to become one with nature and to participate in the process of life itself.

Two epic poems, *The Iliad* and *The Odyssey*, marked the event. *The Iliad* deals with human nature before the birth of thought, when humans were still blindly obedient to their many gods and to the voices and signs that directed them. *The Odyssey* reflects the depth of the changes and the trial by fire that ensued. By 500 B.C., Delphi had lost its hold over the rulers of the times, and one by one the prophets were being silenced. People were developing their own wills. As Homer wrote in *Ulysses*, "What he greatly thought he nobly dared."

The Old Testament recorded the transition. The New Testament spelled out the difference. Trial and error created turmoil and terror in the process. Because the power of thought could be applied for evil as well as for good, people had great difficulty adjusting to its use, and society in general became alarmed over its misuse. It was under these conditions that the moral leaders of the day began to advocate the power of good thoughts, and to caution against the consequence of evil thoughts.

In Paul's letter to the Church at Philippi, he urged the congregation "to think on those things which are true, honest, just, pure, lovely and on all things of good report." The problem, then as now, was how to exercise individual control over thought. Thought out of control, or applied to unworthy goals, could cause illness, injury,

From the Inkwell to the Internet

December 2, 1999

Mr. Nathan M. Shippee
P.O. Box 747
Old Lyme, CT 06371

Dear Mr. Shippee:

    I well remember your visit to our offices a number of years ago, and I thank you for the additional citations for *Human Being* that you have just sent along. We will, of course, add them to our files.

Sincerely yours,

Frederick C. Mish
Vice President and Editor in Chief

FCM/gbb

Merriam-Webster Inc.
47 Federal Street • P.O. Box 281 • Springfield, MA 01102
Telephone (413) 734-3134 • Facsimile (413) 731-5979 • http://www.m-w.com

even end in self-destruction. This was recognized then, and has been the subject of admonitions ever since.

In parable after parable, page after page, the New Testament sets forth moral standards for the new condition, tells of the rise of the new force, of the source of the new power within. It is all there for the understanding of it. It is there in the parable of the talents, in the admonition to love, in the revelation of the power of personal prayer. "The Kingdom of God is within you."

Listen. Look within. Think.

THE TIP OF THE POINT

It was in 600 B.C. that Solon of Athens gave mankind the injunction: Know thyself, first. From Solon to Socrates to Aristotle, from Hebrew thought to Roman thought, the process gathered force. By the end of the first millennium, during the attempted reformation of Judaism by Jesus, sufficient numbers of people had become actively manned to tip the scale, and the power of thought became a dominating force in society.

With the birth of thought, mankind set out on a voyage of discovery. It was a different world in the making, a major evolutionary event. It marked a turning point as much as any other major evolutionary event of the past; from fin to foot to wing to thumb.

The human race embarked on an amazing odyssey, and like Homer's Ulysses, what was greatly thought, was nobly dared. With the birth of thought, the human race emerged as more than an advanced biological species. No longer just part of the inventory, mankind achieved status, became part of nature's management, a trustee with an evolutionary role, with responsibility within the process. With the birth of thought, the human race took on immortality.

With the power of thought, we have opened our minds to the meaning of life. We have awakened our awareness of the eternity of the life process.

With the power of thought, we have conceptualized conscience, soul, and spirit; we have exercised free will, challenged fate, and celebrated life, all with the knowledge that a lifetime is measured by birth and death, but that eternal life lies within. It lies within our thoughts and through our thoughts, within our grasp.

Count the stars; add up the light years from here to there; be impressed by the immensity of the universe. Stir your imagination, and then ask the question: "Is there any point to it?"

Yes, I believe there is a point to it. We are the point, the very tip of the point. I believe that it is important for us to think, to give more thought to the power of thought, for to whatsoever we put our thoughts, we shall become. What we are is the product of what we think, and what we shall be will be shaped by the same process. To think is to create; therefore, choose your thoughts carefully, since they act upon you.

In the process of evolution we are fulfilling a purpose through thinking. Like no other species in the universe, humankind reciprocates the force, which generates the power of thought.

Think on the things you would become. Think on these things.

THINK ON THESE THINGS

Whatsoever things are true,
Whatsoever things are honest,
Whatsoever things are just,
Whatsoever things are pure,
Whatsoever things are lovely,
Whatsoever things are of good report,
Think on these things.

Philippians 4:8
The Letter of Paul to the Church at Philippi

CHAPTER EIGHT

THE MIND

MIND IS DIFFERENT FROM BRAIN. BRAIN IS the physical object we employ in our thinking; mind is the metaphysical element that directs our thinking. "What is mind? No matter. What is matter? Never mind," was the way *Punch* put it at the time that Darwin was making an issue of mind and matter.

Mind is at the interface of reality and possibility. With it, we can monitor the effects of present concepts upon reality, while evaluating the possibilities of advantage through change to new concepts. It is with our mind that we perceive, create, conceptualize, enthuse. It is to our mind that we turn for knowledge. Brain is the object we employ, but mind is the element that directs it, the source of the knowledge.

If we are not careful here, we may answer too quickly, for we have lived so long in the brilliance of scientific discovery, we have come to equate that which is known with knowledge. Under the discipline of science, that which is known has become limited to that which can be proven. If it cannot be proven, it doesn't exist; it is other than knowledge. This narrow definition of knowledge is one of the major obstacles to individual development. This is an obstacle that must be dealt with by educators as a matter of vital concern, because this limited definition stunts our growth, limits our potential, and threatens our destiny as Human Beings; it even suggests that we have no soul because we cannot prove we have one. Held to that concept for too long, we shall come to believe it. Since we become as we think, we then run the risk of forfeiting our soul through disbelief, a very real possibility under the complex rules of emergent evolution.

Just as there are stars in the sky even when not visible in the light of the day, there is knowledge in our minds that may not be known under the scientific definition of knowledge. We can see the stars when the sun goes down. In the same manner, we can expect to know the whole of knowledge when we turn down the brilliance of scientific methodology so that we may also "see" that part of knowledge that lies beyond the material vanishing point at which the physical and the metaphysical join.

What is knowledge? Certainly it is more than we know, more than can be proven. All embracing, knowledge includes the known, the unknown, and the unknowable. Our knowledge is not limited, only not totally realized. With the source of our knowledge in our mind, the limit for us occurs only when we close our minds; in itself, knowledge is infinite.

WHO IS THE KNOWER?

The paradox of knowledge is that it encompasses both the knowables and the unknowables. Consider that for just a moment: not only the known and the unknown, which may become known through research, but also the unknowable, which by definition can never be "known." That is the paradox of knowledge; that is the challenge to educators in their responsibility to young minds, to inquiring minds, to minds thirsting for knowledge.

How to open minds to unlimited knowledge? How to learn technology, study science, engage in research, and also learn to think, to dream, to wonder, to enthuse, to conceptualize, to do all the special, wonderful things a computer cannot do. It is the problem of dimension that confronts us here, for the unknowables are in a different dimension, a non-physical dimension, a metaphysical element of our complex self. We experience the knowables within the dimension of time and space, but we experience the unknowables outside the confines of the physical world. We do not have to prove this; we know it to be so. We are our own authority for this area of knowledge. We are the knower.

I have read, and searched my mind about this invisible area of knowledge for most of my adult years and recently resolved to try a new approach. Knowing that medicine uses a virus to quell a virus led me to employ a paradox to solve a paradox, a chart to chart the unchartable, a diagram to define the un-definable. The question was not to unite, or in some manner reconcile the two. The different dimensions of the physical and

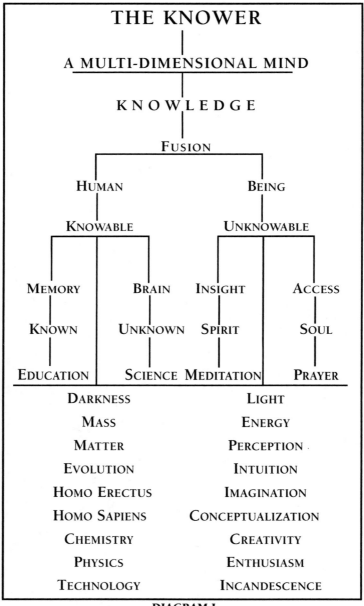

DIAGRAM I

spiritual do not themselves interact. They remain oblivious to each other. The different dimensions interact only through the willpower of the "knower" (who will be referred to hereafter as an individual, personalized and capitalized.) The Knower engages the mind to fuse the physical dimension with the spiritual dimension, and thus creates a new thing: *Being.* Such Being is more than existence; it is the image of God cast into human form with the potential for Becoming, of coming into Being. The mind translates the different languages of the knowables and the unknowables into understanding, and the Knower is thereby able to understand the physical and the metaphysical, and to write poems as well as formulae. Just as we might make hay while the sun shines and dance to music of the night, so we employ our bodily frame for making a living, but engage our God-like intellect for making a life. The Knower knows how to make a living, and also how to make a life. The Knower knows how to draw upon the bottomless well of unlimited knowledge. The Knower knows how to deal with the paradox of the knowables and the unknowables. Diagram 1 is a chart to help you visualize this concept of the unlimited nature of knowledge.

THE LOVE OF KNOWLEDGE

Finding the mind is the most important discovery an individual can make. Once real access is gained, the mind is never lost. As the poets and philosophers know so well, when the mind is opened, there begins a love affair with knowledge. This love embraces the whole broad spectrum of knowledge, a harmonious, balanced equilibrium of knowledge, like a rainbow in full arc, with living colors.

Knowledge becomes indistinguishable from self once the mind is opened. Self-knowledge becomes the range of one's understanding, knowing something with familiarity. The pursuit of knowledge leads on to a search of basic truths. We grow as our minds grow. We do not grow with years. With years we merely get older. Maturity develops as we learn to grow with the mind. We respond more by a challenge to the mind than we do by a challenge to the brain. Monetary income is sufficient for the work of the brain, but the work of the mind wants psychic income, a source of satisfaction, a sense of joy, love, peace.

Once you have found your own mind, embrace it, never let it go. Develop your mind; put it to work at the frontier of your knowledge. Open new sections of your mind, and develop each further. Learn how to make more than a living. Learn how to make a life.

Take another look at Diagram I, the diagram of the Knower. Take a balanced look at it. Read once more the left side, and then the right side, and let your mind be the fulcrum, the axis that also supplies your capability for action. Stand on two legs, include both sides, and feel the strength of your own knowing, since self-assurance, like self-knowledge, comes naturally to all who have full access to their own mind.

AGAINST THE WIND

We have been sailing against the wind of popular belief up to this point, and its velocity has risen until all have heard the wind howl its persistent wail: "Prove it." But winds calm down, and weather changes. It seems to me that we are experiencing a weather change now. We are entering a calmer period of reflection. If this is so, then we should make the most of it and take full advantage of it. Our times are Human Rights times, times of individual freedom, meaning the freedom to think, to speak, and to be. We are reaching for the freedom not just to exist, but to Be, to come into Being.

Our time is a time of self-constructibility, for we become as we think. It is within this context that we speak of the Knower, and look deeper into the dimensions of knowledge. But we are not yet out of the weather, for the winds still howl around us: "Prove it. If it can't be proven, it doesn't exist."

AS IT IS

Science conducts a search for truth through factual observations with experiments, the results of which do not change when repeated. Philosophy conducts a search for truth through reasoning rather than factual observation. Let us digress for a moment to look at each separately, and observe whether either can survive alone. Let us analyze Diagram I in that context and make an individual judgment. Can science and philosophy survive separation?

NO MIND — ONLY MATTER

Just as the brain has two hemispheres, each with individually different aspects, so does knowledge. What happens if from our Diagram I we have access to one column only? Let's try a modified diagram, and call Diagram II The Learner. This diagram is readily recognizable because we have been brought up on it. It's fairly representative of our educational system today. We draw upon our computer-like brain for knowledge. We function as if we have no mind, only gray matter. Our system of education puts a premium on cultivating memory to acquire knowledge of the known, and look to science to increase knowledge by bringing the unknowns into the known. Everything else is considered to be outside the total of knowledge. No wonder we need alcohol and drugs to dull our minds, and aspirin to aid us in living within the confines of this one side. That there are exceptions among us only proves the rule; in general, we have learned to live within the confines of this diagram for the most part.

This type of limited knowledge is called "software processing" in the computer trade, and the output of the software depends on the input. There is a computer trade quip, which makes this point vivid: "garbage in — garbage out." When all of our knowledge is limited to that which can be programmed-in, and proven through repetition under factual observations, then we are dealing with regurgitated material for which the odoriferous word "garbage" is not inappropriate.

Let's look for what is missing in Diagram II. Where are spirit and soul? Where is creativeness? Where did the source of moral values — perception, enthusiasm, incandescence, energy, light — disappear to? How do we develop and grow without concepts? Is there nothing to meditate about, no God to hear our prayers?

Ethical principles have their origin somewhere outside absolute reality. Why does a person do a "right" thing? What motivates a person to follow conscience? The answers cannot be found in Diagram II. Our sense of values, especially moral values, is derived from a deeper well than the brain, deeper than any part of the bodily frame. Our sense of moral values is derived from our spirituality. It is from this well that each draws self-knowledge, and materializes the concept of self-constructibility.

We become stunted if we permit ourselves to remain within the confines of Diagram II. The possibility of interaction between science and philosophy is denied, and the denial dampens our incandescence, which is the inner light of spirit. The embers become ash, and darkness descends upon us. The destiny of coming into Being is lost, and no worthwhile destiny is offered to replace it. "God is dead," is the curse Nietzche hurled at life. Death is accepted as *termination*, not seen as *graduation*. We accept ourselves as Homo sapiens without free will, without the freedom to become, destined to stay limited.

BLITHE SPIRIT

Man may not live by bread alone, but it sure beats going hungry. We do have a bodily frame, but we also have a god-like intellect. What would happen if we directed our thoughts only to it? If we were to take the same relative position as philosophers that scientists take in dissecting knowledge, and focused solely upon our god-like intellects, we would be in just as awkward a position, only we wouldn't have to suffer long, for lack of nourishment would soon end the ecstasy. This is made clear in Diagram III, The Seeker.

This diagram provides little nourishment for the bodily frame, but it gives full rein to the soul and spirit. Fasting is an affirmation akin to this, and fasting is often related to an intense religious experience. Like lightning, the pure light of weightless insight associated with Diagram III is highly visible, but not containable for long in human form. But it is useful to examine Diagram III, and to ponder its meaning, because it reveals our potential if joined with our physical mass, while disclosing our limitation when denied. Whether Blithe Spirit or Solely Scientific, none of us need stand alone; rather, each is a part, none apart.

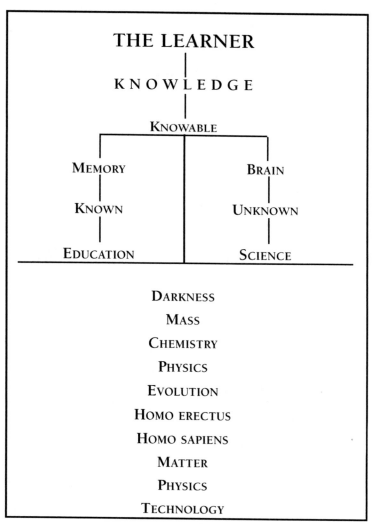

DIAGRAM II

One, a part of all
All, none apart
One and all a total fabric
A universal field of energy
Alternating, ebbing, flowing
Ever moving ...

Man a part
A part, none apart
We reciprocate the movement
Within ourselves
Of cosmic energy
Ebbing, flowing, ever moving

Man positioned
At the balance point
Cosmic Force
Stirring our Being
Setting in Motion
This force of conscience

Mind over mind,
Thoughts in motion
No other generator
In the universe,
Man alone produces
The power of conscience.

"The Knower"
Nathan M. Shippee, 1978

WE CAN CHANGE

The case for the mind being more than protein was advanced by a professor of molecular biophysics, Harold J. Morowitz. He attacked Carl Sagan's thesis in his book, *The Dragons of Eden,* this way:

> "In addition to being weak, it is a dangerous view since the way we respond to our fellow human beings is dependent on the way we conceptualize them. To see ourselves as animals or machines can become a self-fulfilling prophecy."

I wanted to include an observation by a scientist about a scientist because I do not want to appear to be opposed to science, but how much more effective would it have been if Professor Morowitz had used initial caps on Human Being! It is the singularity of science, and its tendency towards totalitarian control over knowledge that we consider objectionable, not science per se. We can modify the singularity of science, and by doing so we can change its materialistic emphasis on life, but we must fortify the determination of our educators to do so, for it is over education that science tends to exercise its way. In its rightful place, science is irreplaceable, but not as judge and jury. That is the place of the Knower.

If we accept this premise, change must begin in our educational system. Education must make room for meditation; mass must be leavened with energy; physics must be lightened with perception. Knowledge must be the fruit of the whole mind. The mind must be kept open. What would change if we changed? What would we add to our thoughts if we opened our minds to our spiritual origin and our thoughts to that part of knowledge that includes the unknowables, the extra dimension of Being? We can change.

We are creative. We create. Through the power of thought we create new forms of material, even new forms of life. More importantly, we are also the object of our creative abilities. We work upon ourselves. Through the power of our thoughts, we become as we think.

Look again at Diagram I, The Knower. Open the mind to the knowables, and to the unknowables; become a Knower. Look for the balance point of every question; look for the harmony in every concept. Without balance and harmony, there will continue to be discord and failure. Keep an open mind and think about these things, for we do become as we think.

THE HUMAN BEING

In the end, this book is not about *origins*, but about *destinations*. Human Beings are inherently revolutionary. We are the only contents that sets itself the task of redesigning the container. This emergent property of self-constructability has a danger zone, which we must guard against where excessive pride or naked willfulness can take over, as we have witnessed during the 20th Century.

Luigi Pirandello (1869-1936), one of the most powerful dramatists of the 1900's, pioneered the concept of, we become as we think in his play "*It Is So! (If You Think*

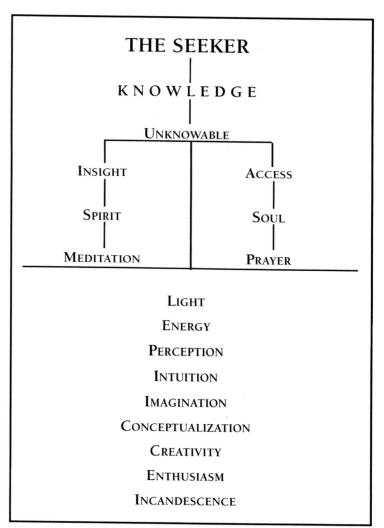

THE SEEKER
|
K N O W L E D G E
|
UNKNOWABLE

INSIGHT   ACCESS

SPIRIT   SOUL

MEDITATION   PRAYER

LIGHT

ENERGY

PERCEPTION

INTUITION

IMAGINATION

CONCEPTUALIZATION

CREATIVITY

ENTHUSIASM

INCANDESCENCE

DIAGRAM III

So). His portrayal of the struggle for life in its inner essence is as fresh as today's playwright's themes that life is more than its private depths. The concept lives on and it has taken fresh meaning since the end of the cold war, with international focus on individuals, on the people. Given today's 24/7 cycle of global mass media, the danger zone has been raised to an alert stage and it will not lessen with time. However, it can be held in check by a concerned citizenry of Human Beings whose combined conscience will not tolerate its abuse.

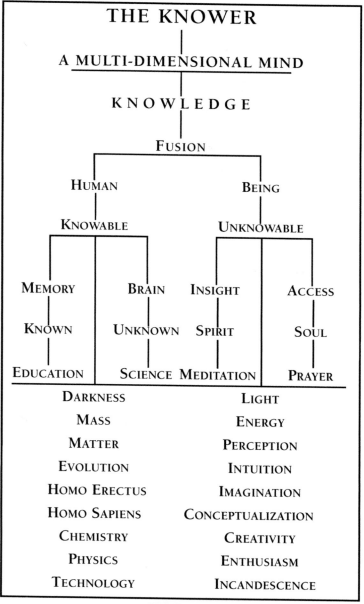

DIAGRAM I

Evolution Evolves;
We Become As We Think

— *Nathan Shippee*

CHAPTER NINE

EVOLUTION EVOLVES

S MART ANIMALS OR HUMAN BEINGS? THE choice is ours. It is ours to decide. We have supplanted natural selection. We have revolutionized evolution. Complexity has accelerated emergence, and new forms are in ascendance. Within a few hundred years, we may exist inside fiber optics, our entire luminous digital bits scattered through all eternity. It is ours to decide. We have the power. Do we have the wisdom? We become as we think.

FROM ORIGINS TO DESTINATIONS

Darwin conceptualized the theory of evolution and wrote about his findings on plant and animal life. He titled his book *Origin of the Species*.

Darwin focused on origins because, for Darwin, evolution was in the past tense. However, the process of evolution is an ongoing, active process. Evolution evolves. Evolution is inventive. Evolution continues. We investigate the process and witness its development. The mind emerges as distinguished exclusively from the body. We look beyond origins toward destination. More than body, we investigate the process of evolution itself with our mind.

The quest is no longer *Where did we come from?* but rather *Where are we bound?* Smart Animals was an earlier stage. Wise Beings is the stage now. In the course of evolution within our time, the species name Homo sapiens has been replaced through the development of the mind by the species Human Beings.

MANKIND'S CHALLENGE

The undeniable influence of Darwin's origins continues to cloud our vision. Origins can be proven, whereas destination is a matter of vision. Science and philosophy vie for our thoughts in determining our destiny. We have become the referee of our own fate. Now, evolution has not been decided by natural selection, but by us. Do we have the wisdom to save ourselves? The power yes, but the wisdom? That is the challenge that Mankind faces at this crucial junction in evolution. It is going to be interesting to witness the actual unfolding of our global society as it takes form.

KNOW THYSELF, FIRST!

In 600 B.C., Solon of Athens gave Mankind the injunction: **know thyself, first**. Solon was the revolutionary who shook things up. Socrates was the philosopher who followed years later. Between them, the Greeks laid the groundwork for the emergence of the mind at a critical stage in evolution. From 600 B.C. to Darwin's time, the focus on the mind produced rich results as libraries flourished, music and poetry ascended and society grew with the spirit of exploration and development. All this changed when, in the 1850's, Darwin's theory of evolution gripped the thoughts of people around the world, from philosophers to even the illiterate, and the focus of Mankind became the image of the ape. Science turned our focus to the body over the mind. The 150 years since has seen little to change the focus. Scientific research has dwelt upon origins to the delight of the public, while philosophy has found only a small audience for destination.

Robert Wright's *The Moral Animal* and Fidelity Funds' slogan, "There Are Bulls and There Are Bears — But You Are a Thinking Animal" set the theme in the early 2000's. Know thyself, first was no longer cool. The mind was not on anyone's mind, it would seem, until the improbable happened and the whole world woke up on 9/11/01 to a new age — the Age of Terror.

Instantly, self-questioning confronted individuals everywhere. Life changed, deeply and dramatically. New values emerged as individuals sought identification. "I'm a Human Being" became an immediate symbol of a new society facing terrorism. Other social and religious forms offered labels that set them apart, but the human psyche sought a universal theme. Human Beings emerged in the social consciousness as the proper image, very different from the image of the ape. The time for the philosopher's voice to be heard was at hand.

The urgent need to rediscover the ancient notion of the philosopher as an individual, as the individual within each of us, the one who exercises wisdom along with power, had become a critical issue. The goal became, as it was in antiquity, to retrain us as Human Beings.

It took a millennium to break down philosophy from a way of life into 'The Age of the Professors,' so termed by Pierre Hadot[13]. It was during the Middle Ages, with the growth of universities, that philosophy lost its connection to lived experience and became entirely an abstract, interpretive enterprise. The love of words took the place of the love of wisdom. This idea of a philosophy reduced to its conceptual context has continued into our own times.

The classical, university conception of philosophy is no longer valid to deal with the challenge individuals face today. The basic admonition Know Thyself, First which was engraved above the entrance at Delphi, is, once again, the wisdom for individuals to apply to our new times. Individuals have the power and now they are applying the wisdom as philosophers of what is right; philosophy as a way of life.

THE BROAD SWEEP OF TIME

In the broad sweep of time, evolution can be viewed in several stages. Here it is divided into six broad stages, counting the past, the present and the future.

The first stage could be named **The Fin**, where life in the waters began to take recognizable form. When the form reached out to land, the second stage of evolution could be called **The Foot**, this over billions of years in terms of our time. Then, eons later, flight emerged; this third stage could be called **The Wing**. The fourth stage came within our recorded history (within the history Darwin dealt with). It could be called **The Thumb**. Science has given the species name Homo sapiens to this stage.

From tens of thousands of years as Homo sapiens to twenty-five hundred years as Human Beings is the time lapse of particular interest to us. In approximately 600 B.C. we could identify the emergence of the power of the mind as a dominating force in human society. From Solon of Athens to Socrates to Aristotle to Hebrew thought, to Roman thought, the process gathered force. By the end of the first millenium, during the attempted reformation of Judaism by Jesus, sufficient numbers of people had become actively manned to tip the scale, and the power of thought took form. With the birth of thought, Mankind set out on a voyage of discovery. A different world was in the making, a major evolutionary event. It marked the turning point as much as the other four major evolutionary events of the past ... from fin to foot to wing to thumb ... and now to mind.

THE MIND

From vassal into vessel, we have been changed dramatically through the birth of thought. Perhaps it is too recent a development to have gained the recognition it merits. Even Darwin failed to convey its significance when he titled his second book, "The Descent of Man."

More recently, Bronowski came closer to focus our attention with his title, "The Ascent of Man." Bronowski did, however, develop the thesis of the uniqueness of Mankind in the development of evolution. Had he added only one more letter to the title of his book to "The Nascent of Man," he would have conveyed that which happened so recently in terms of evolutionary time. For it was our coming into Being that we associate with the birth of thought, the nascence of an eternal life process within the biological life process. It is necesasry to understand the significance of what happened if we are to appreciate that this event was a change in the very nature of the human race.

When Mankind became manned, nature revealed her secrets. Through the power of thought, the unseen atom was visualized, the building blocks of life were translated into chemical formulae and travel to distant stars became as certain as used to be the nomadic journey of the herdsmen from season to season.

Evolution evolved, the process continued and the mind took charge. No longer subject to natural selection or a blind watchmaker, Mankind became responsible for the ongoing development of evolution, for better or worse, for all to witness. For the first time, evolution would not be primarily physical in nature; it would be a transformation of consciousness. Mankind had become a conscious participant in the unfolding and direction of the evolutonary process itself. From now on, if we are to have a future, we must create the future ourselves, for we become as we think. Becoming is our destiny and our thoughts are its engine. We have the power. Do we have the wisdom?

WE

Charles Lindbergh titled his adventurous book "We." This referred to his mind and his machine working together, each alongside the other, one-alongside-one, the equation I think of as "eleven." Successful people are elevens because they embrace the power within. The word "enthusiasm" speaks to this power in the meaning of its Greek origin: entheos, God within.

No longer will nature, in its groping way, propel us through one stage after another. We, as individuals, are the future. We are the revolution. We are the tip of the point of change. It is no longer a mindless world. It is a world that has generated the mind, the mind that now has to define destination, to determine where we are bound.

The goal is not merely to transcend the world, but to transform the world, to become an agent of the development itself. The notion that evolution is a biological event deeply affetcs our understanding of what it means to be human. It is the unexamined consequence of that notion that will shape our future in the long term and will also touch our souls. As Teilard said: *"This is why the cosmic enterprise now hangs on our decision. We are evolution!"*

As we embrace our minds and imagine our future, we sense that we are on the cusp of the next stage of life. In order for this to happen, it will be necessary for us to share our energy — not just our physical energy, or biological energy, but our energy of caring and loving and willing. It is this most intimate energy of ours that must be committed to our new world. We must give of ourselves as individuals in order to create a higher level of life. The challenge is whether Human Beings will actually accomplish this well enough to bring about a higher level of cosmic evolution.

SYMBOLS

A symbol is of great importance and of real worth. It provides a way for the individual to see and to understand the outer world in a way that would not be possible without the particular symbol. It illustrates the world for the individual. Having this special quality, the symbol is "alive," and opens up beyond itself, touching something which the understanding does not fully encompass, but into which it wishes to reach. Then the symbol becomes social, and it takes on the function of holding large groups together."

– Dr. C.G.Jung
Zurich

CHAPTER TEN

THE SYMBOL OF UPPERCASE

S YMBOLS ARE NOT CONTRIVED, THEY ARE spontaneous and must well up from within. What new energy dormant in our psyche lies waiting to supplant Homo sapiens and to take the monkey off our backs? What would change if we changed the symbol for Mankind? What would a slight change in our self-esteem do for our attitudes toward everything we do?

Upper case is a symbol that is used for emphasis and for respect. Lower and upper case create a vital distinction in vocabulary, and in the definition of words and their meaning. Lower case for human being is a word, but upper case Human Being is the proper noun for us. We do not use lower case "i". We use upper case "I". We use *I* as a proper noun for each of us.

The proposal of upper case for Human Being was first published during an interview with me in 1979. The occasion was a discussion of my book, *Becoming*, during which the question of human destiny was raised. I responded:

"I'm looking for a unifying concept, a symbol that will come alive within others as it has within me. That's why I picked up on upper case Human Being. A Human Being is not any denomination, or race, or sex. If we can link an individual with the universe it would be a great contribution to society."

The idea that upper case for Human Being would raise the self-esteem of individuals everywhere, and simultaneously raise the level of society and improve the well-being of all, seemed absurd to many at that time. But this did not arrest it. "If at first the idea is not absurd then there is no hope for it" was the way Albert Einstein addressed it.

The idea was being advanced in different ways around the world. Roger Rosenblatt wrote a remarkable essay for the February 21, 1983, issue of *Time* on the Commission Report of the Beirut massacre, which he titled, "The Law of the Mind". He pointed out that, "the power of the report goes beyond Israel. It is an expression of moral thought which holds that there is a secret truth in human actions which bears equal weight and status with objectively provable reality.

"What this says about human nature," wrote Mr. Rosenblatt, "is that one cannot escape his own knowledge. Gunfire is real, but so are thoughts. Hatred in the mind caused slaughter in the streets."

In 2000, the United Nations carried the idea forward on many fronts, culminating in the International

Commission on Intervention and State Sovereignty, which took up the question of humanitarian intervention. The idea that national leaders who abuse citizens can no longer escape reckoning by hiding behind national sovereignty raised the question to a new level of the issue between human rights and national rights. Yugoslavia made the headlines with the Hague Tribunal for Bosnia war crimes, followed by the national uprising which overthrew President Milosovic and brought in a new constitution. The arrest of Chile's Pinochet brought the focus to South America, but Africa remained off the radar screen. The United Nations' failure to act in Rawanda became viewed as a blatant act of racism. Canada's Foreign Minister Lloyd Axworthy offered to pay for a program within the United Nations to study the implications. "Our take has been that since the end of the cold war we have to focus on individuals, on the people."

THE PATH IT TOOK

The autonomy of the individual began in recent history with the explorers as the pathfinders whose exploits began the slow process of igniting the conscience of their people. The legend of Robin Hood; the Knights of the Round Table; the rise of the English Parliament; the American Colonies and the Western Frontier; the democratization of Europe; the spread of democracy slowly everywhere were all markers along the path to autonomy of the individual over the past millennium. In the 20th Century, two World Wars accelerated the pace

200,000 Rally to Mark Opposition Victory

"The genie of freedom and democracy has escaped from the bottle and it's impossible to push it back in."

Zarko Trebjesanin, psychologist

"Thousands of people flash 3-finger salutes during an opposition rally Wednesday in Belgrade. The crowd swarmed the capital's main square protesting Yugoslav President Slobodan Milosevic's efforts to avoid an electoral defeat."

Emil Vas, Associated Press

of the rise of the individual in whom all decisions would be finally vested.

In the 1930's one individual in Germany seized upon the concept of self-constructability with naked willfulness and brought about the horror of National Socialism through an evil doctrine emphasizing the exaggerated pride of a Super Race. We have been endowed with a power of self-constuctability both as individuals and national leaders, for evil as well as for good. The challenge that Hitler gave the world was how to ensure against the huge danger of being Super Anything and avoid shipwreck through the evil dictates of a single leader.

In 1945, the United Nations was formed by the victorious nations. It was open to all nations that would subscribe to the Charter. A milestone in the Charter of the United Nations was the Declaration of Human Rights, which formed the foundation upon which the autonomy of the individual has since relied.

The Nuremberg Trials of War Criminals in 1950 brought a new element of individual responsibility to the public conscience, which continued to grow until the Millennium Celebration of the United Nations in New York. It was there that the right to intervene to save citizens even if that meant intruding on national sovereignty was promulgated. Three years earlier, the armed forces of 19 nations had intervened in the national sovereignty of Yugoslavia to end the ethnic cleansing in Bosnia. The citizens of Yugoslavia themselves rose up in October 2000 to remove their leader and expunge the status of isolation he had forced upon them.

As the 21st Century dawned, the autonomy of individual Human Rights was an accepted status, and a violator, whether an individual or a nation, would be pursued and punished. Individuals everywhere began to take notice of themselves as individuals of worth, with meaning. The status of upper case had begun with the Declaration of Human Rights in the United Nations Charter, and it would be a short step to give the same status of privilege to Human Beings.

A Human Being is an individual not limited to race or creed, to gender or individual circumstance. A Human Being is unlimited in every sense. Each individual who thinks of himself as a Human Being may aspire to the rank of Human Being and wear the mantle of Humanitarian. Each will make his or her own judgment. Some have said that this is just a play on words or merely semantics. But we become as we think, and who we think we are is determinate. The proper words can clear our thoughts, and clear thoughts can clear our path ahead.

GETTING THERE WAS HALF THE FUN

The location of the United Nations Headquarters in New York City brought a concentration of world leaders who became involved in the culture of the area in addition to their responsibilities in the world body. In 1980, following the publication of *BECOMING: Coming Into Being,* I attended meetings with several Ambassadors who had particular interest in the Declaration of Human Rights. In the course of expanding upon that concept, a series of discussion groups was held at Pace University in New York City to expand upon the idea of the autonomy of the individual existing independently of the state, with self-directing freedom, especially moral independence. The concept was that the model of humanity should be an ideal, not an average. A standard of perfection should be the ultimate object of endeavor.

A progression of thoughts that emerged from these discussions suggested a vital concern with Being that implied a prospect beyond mere existence. Being also implies movement toward a destination.

The early meetings began with a service held at Pace University, at which the heads of six university departments, including English, Philosophy, History, Psychology, Religion, and Arts, spoke on related topics and answered questions.

On April 2, 1980, the Director of Graduate Programs and Public Administration, S.J. Prezioso, followed up the meeting with a proposal that Pace University sponsor an International Conference on the Destination of Human Beings. As news of the proposal began to take hold, it became clear that a location with overnight facilities would be needed to accommodate the respondents. A Conference Center in Tarrytown, New York, was selected and preparations began in earnest, among them, a Roper Poll of ten questions to 2,000 individuals across the United States.

Four Topic Areas were issued as part of the Conference Program, including:

1. **The accelerating rise of self-aware-ness among individuals every-where, and their willingness to take risks as part of their search for a new pattern of commitment to life.**

2. **The need to defuse the continuing controversy over different thoughts on "origin" and the related ques-tion regarding "destination."**

3. **A proposed Amendment to the United Nations Declaration of Human Rights to apply upper case to Human Being therein.**

4. **A broader role for education, in order to accommodate the thirst for free inquiry.**

All of the thoughts projected a vital concern with Being, and a direction toward a destination. The ques-tion was asked, "Toward what destination is the Destination Conference to move?" The consensus was to move toward the clarification of thought. It was appar-ent that the controversy over "origins" had clouded thoughts and obscured vision. It was reasonable to expect that by enlarging our focus to include destina-tion, we would encourage constructive thoughts and sharpen vision. Since we become as we think, what we think is important to what we become.

Once preparations were underway with the encouragement of Pace University, other avenues of public awareness were approached. A proposed Amendment to the United Nations Declaration of Human Rights to apply upper case to Human Being therein began by enlisting the aid of several ambassadors, including Jose M. Chaves, Ambassador to the Spanish-speaking Nations. In the summer of 1981, Ambassador Chaves sponsored a Resolution in the General Assembly that would amend the First Article of the Declaration of Human Rights to capitalize the initial letters of Human Being whenever that term was used in the Declaration, and in all texts published by the United Nations. The given purpose was to "enhance the dignity of Human Beings."

The effort to amend the Declaration was carried forward on a broad scale, both with the Secretary General, and with many of the member ambassadors whose countries must vote to amend the Charter. On August 7, 1980, the Secretary General Kurt Waldheim was addressed on the matter, and a reply on August 19, 1980 was received from Lottie Robins, Chief of Public Inquiries. On November 10, 1980, a Resolution was submitted to the General Assembly for consideration.

Much praise was received as a result of the efforts being made at the United Nations with its high profile supporters, but a majority vote in the General Assembly for an amendment to the Charter was never achieved for the unforeseen reason that many of the world languages do not have lower and upper case.

UNITED NATIONS   Distr.

GENERAL ASSEMBLY
NOVEMBER 10, 1980

_____Session
Agenda Item_____

HUMAN RIGHTS RESOLUTION

Question related to the dignity of the Human Being as set forth in the First Article of the Declaration of Human Rights.

The General Assembly

Recognition of the relationship of the status of a Human Being to the dignity of a Human Being, and the consequential right of a Human Being to the use of initial caps in the correct spelling of the proper name *Human Being*.

Decides that the Declaration of Human Rights of the United Nations be, and is amended by correcting the spelling of Human Being from lower case to initial caps in Article One, and thereafter throughout all of the usage in all of the texts of the United Nations to more properly reflect the dignity of the Human Being, and the entitlement of the Human Being to the status of a proper name.

A TIGER BY THE TAIL

While the negotiations were underway at the United .Nations, parallel efforts were moving with the dictionary publishers and the press. The publishers were identified as a principal target because, incredible as it may seem, they had no definition for *human being*. There was no separate listing for human being, only a buried inclusion under the definition for Homo sapiens.

A series of visits and letters to the five dictionary companies began in 1983 in order to evaluate their procedures and try to accommodate them. It became evident early on that the requirement was common usage. But, since they were in control of common usage, and its source of ultimate correctness, the press, editors and authors everywhere were compelled to use human being as a species of Homo sapiens, lower case and all.

This dilemma was set forth by Merriam-Webster's letter of September 7, 1983, in which the Editorial Director wrote:

> "I should tell you first of all that it is not, in our views, the function of dictionaries to promulgate or promote new words and meanings but rather to record those that have already established themselves in widespread and frequent use and that dictionary users are therefore likely to look up at need."

The efforts were undiminished over the years, as is documented in the correspondence with Merriam-

Webster and the other dictionary companies. On February 23, 1984, Merriam-Webster wrote:

> "Thanks for the citations for "Human Being," capital letters and all, which we will certainly add to our citation files."

In September 1984 Merriam-Webster acknowledged additional examples of Human Being and wrote: "Thank you for another citation for Human Being. We will add it to our files." And again on December 2, 1999, their 150th Anniversary Year, Merriam-Webster (From the Inkwell to the Internet) wrote:

> "I well remember your visit to our offices a number of years ago, and I thank you for the additional citiations for Human Being that you have sent along. We will, of course, add them to our files."

ENTER THE INTERNET

At the same time, on October 18, 1999, the *Oxford English Dictionary* entered the electronic world of the Internet with a global appeal for new words, new usages, new senses, spellings or pronunciations. The appeal went on to state:

> "Oxford leads the field in recording the entry of today's new words into the language. We need readers' help to find printed evidence of new words from magazines, newspapers, books, song lyrics, practical manuals — indeed from any published source, slang and dialect words are also collected. New senses or usages of an existing word, an unusual spelling are all welcome."

We were prompt in sending a sampling of citations for Human Being beginning with the 1887 use in the Preface of *Sylvia and Bruno,* by Lewis Carroll, the 1984 novel by Molly Keane, *Time after Time*, and a variety of citations from the Pace University Destination Conference and the press coverage that it spawned. The entries to the *Oxford English Dictionary* were, in turn, sent to the five American dictionaries as further evidence for their citation files.

Removing the enigma of the "dictionary-less word" was a milestone, and a fitting finish to the 20th Century. Human Being entered the 21st Century with recognition of the *Oxford English Dictionary* and the status of a personal pronoun. We were on the Internet, and we were global.

FINISHING TOUCHES

In addition to the United Nations and the dictionary companies as target areas, the television outlets were also addressed. One in particular in the New York region was the Public Broadcasting Station Channel Thirteen, which ran a series on *The Brain* and on *The Mind*. The station was approached with the proposal to continue with *The Soul*, but was gently turned down with the rejoinder: "The problem is that the soul — as you so eloquently point out — can in no way be studied from the point of view of science."

The problem that Channel Thirteen had in 1988 with science and with soul was akin to the problem that education was having between scientific evolution and creationist evolution, which finally boiled over in Kansas when the Board of Education in 1998 voted to remove evolution from the curriculum. When faced with a public outcry from the technology community over a perceived economic backlash, the current board members were voted out, and science was voted back in the year 2000.

The fight to keep the theory of evolution as part of the science curriculum in schools by many states has been led by the National Center for Science Education. One of the leaders in the scientific community, who holds fast to his personal soul while pursuing his professionalism in science, is Dr. Kenneth R. Miller,

Professor of Biology & Medicine at Brown University. His book, *Finding Darwin's God,* was published at the end of 1999. Our proposal to mediate the conflict between the "creationists" and the scientific community in a Win-Win Forum setting was not accepted on the grounds that:

> "Unfortunately, having read scores of books and articles by so-called "scientific creationists," I can assure you they have nothing to do with your ideas. Sorry to be so frank, but that is exactly how your offer would be received."

The slogan of the Win-Win Forum was *Not Whether Right Or Wrong, But How To Get Along.* We viewed Human Being as a Win-Win Solution because it involves the interaction between the contents and the container, each part a part of the whole. The Diagram I in Chapter VIII illustrates the interaction of scientific knowledge and creationist faith within the multidimensional intelligence of the Human Being. We felt that the Win-Win Forum could be useful in the resolution of the conflict, and it would afford us with another avenue to public awareness.

A DIFFERENT THING

Trying to persuade the dictionary companies to include Human Being as a new word was one level of effort. Opening a dialog with the Vatican was a different thing.

In 1987, diplomatic channels were explored in New York City with the Office of Communications of the Arch Diocese. A noted video producer, Alvin Cooperman, who had directed a video on the life story of Pope John Paul II at the Vatican, offered help. A breakfast meeting on April 21, 1987, was arranged with Monsignor Flynn, who acknowledged the proposition in his letter that day in closing with, "I shall get back to you on the 'Human Being' soon."

A package of documents and information was forwarded to the Vatican. The King James version of the Bible had included human being as a substitute for the gender words of his, her, him, to remove the element of sexism from the Bible. Our point was to elevate all genders to Human Beings. Eleven years later, a response was received from the Vatican dated November 12, 1998, which said:

> "I am directed to acknowledge the letter and enclosures which you have sent to His Holiness Pope John Paul II, and I would assure you that the contents have been noted."

WE BECOME AS WE THINK

Over history, the human mind has sought out truth. Solon, in ancient times, put it this way: "Know thyself, first."

The *Talmud*, speaking of wine, put it this way: "Examine the contents, Not the bottle."

When Descartes said, "I think therefore I am," there was always the unfinished question: "I am what? To me, the answer was apparent: "I am to think!"

We are to think. That is what Chapter VII is about. *The Birth of Thought* is an important chapter in our life here. That is the hallmark of the Human Being. Through the power of our thoughts, we work upon ourselves. We ourselves are the object of our creative abilities. The possibilities for good through a change in our self-image are open to us.

Developing a definition for Human Being may provide our real missing link. The Millennium has brought change. Leading up to the Millennium were events heralding change. The new autonomy of the individual is prominent in these changes. The individual feels the change and seeks an identity within it.

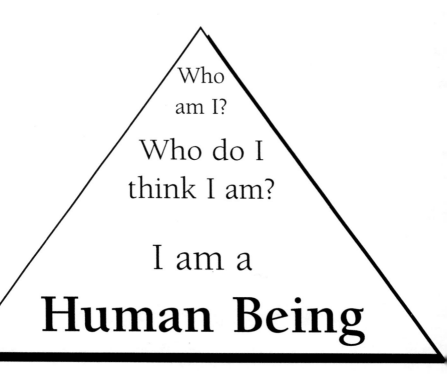

133

APPENDIX

From time to time, the Human Being Foundation will issue supplementary essays to its members.

This is one of a series of supplemental essays.

CHANGE THE RULES...CHANGE THE GAME (DARWIN CHANGED THE GAME)

"WE HAVE TO KNOW THAT WE COME WITH A SET OF DIRECTIONS!"

The advance copy of THE HUMAN BEING has brought a depth of response and enlightenment that wants to be shared. One, in particular, touches on the central theme: RULES RULE. We need to change the rules to change the game.

"NATHAN! I just finished THE HUMAN BEING and need to tell you how much I enjoyed it.

I don't know who we are, where we come from, but it is very clear to me that it matters and I think about the answers. I suspect we don't need to know it all, but MUST know that it matters. We have to know that we come with a set of directions.

Your book makes it clear to me we need to pay attention to them. We are given "wake-up calls" in different ways. Your writing is your way of sharing your "wake-up call."

DARWIN CHANGED THE GAME

Everyone knows that we are Human Beings, but that is not what we are taught. From kindergarten to 12th grade, we are taught that we are of mammalian descent – species name: Homo sapiens...smart animals. It all began 150 years ago, when Charles Darwin published his scientific theory title THE DESCENT OF MAN and continues to flourish today.

The concept that we are biologically related to the apes is an obstacle that clouds our thinking and belittles our self-image. We are made to seem less than we really are – and that matters!

A CHANGE IS NEEDED!

Darwin's theory is a pressing issue, as Kansas and Ohio have recently illustrated. Advocates of biological evolution vie with advocates of spiritual evolution in establishing rules for the teaching of evolution as science. It goes back and forth, but science always wins: WE ARE DESCENDED FROM THE APES!

The problem with this situation is that the two sides are fighting each other rather than facing the reality that "evolution" evolves. Whatever something was may have changed and may keep on changing. The significance of this is that we are self-constructable — we influence change — we become as we think.

If we think only along Darwin's theory, we become ape-like in our conduct and in our thoughts. If we broaden our thinking — think with our mind rather than just with our brain — we become who we really are...Human Beings — upper case and all.

WHO MAKES THE RULES?

As one Massachusetts politician once said: "Everything is local." It all begins in the community, at the school board level, where textbooks are purchased and students are taught to think. The tug-of-war began in 1925 with the Scopes trial over the teaching of biological evolution as science. It intensified over the issue of diving design, which introduced the problem of separation of church and state. The result of this was Hobson's choice of evolution as science. It did not allow evolution to evolve; it merely avoided the issue of religion.

The other side of a problem is an opportunity. The other side of this problem becomes awareness of the evolution of the mind. The mind is the essence that sets us apart from biological evolution. This is the essence that gave us the ability to rise above the level of Homo sapiens and become Human Beings. This is what the rules change is all about — and it matters!

THE BUTTERFLY EFFECT

When a butterfly flutters its wings in one part of the world, it can eventually cause a hurricane in another.

To the extent that our local school boards limit the teacher of our children to biological evolution – that we are descended from the apes – they will tend to hold this image as their guide. To start our youth on such a path is to stunt their growth, for as the branch is bent so the tree will grow.

If, at the local level, we can expand the horizon and accept that evolution evolves, it could be the force that would change the way we think at all levels of society – worldwide. Even a small change in the way we think will make a big change in the way we act. It is all in the mind.

OUR GOAL – A FIVE YEAR PLAN!

THE HUMAN BEING FOUNDATION has a FIVE YEAR PLAN designed to establish Foundation Centers in 300 communities in 50 states to connect with like-minded pioneers in one-on-one discourse about our place in life – species name: Human Beings. At some point within the five-year span, a tipping point will occur and a surge will swell that lifts all before it, as a tide lifts all ships at sea.

Just as surely as nature evolves, the freeing of minds will change attitudes and peace will no longer be written on parchment because it will be embossed in the minds of Mankind.

It is not too ambitious to think that the result of a rule change at the local school board level will change the world. Darwin did it with one book 150 years ago, with his theory of the decent of man that changed the game for the mind of man. We can get a good start on opening our minds during the next five years by restating the rules of the game and returning our self-esteem to the path of good health.

BECOME INVOLVED – LEND A HELPING HAND

Since you have read this far, don't stop now! We want to hear from you. How to become an Associate? How to become a Member? How to be a pioneer and open a Foundation Center in your community?

Please write to: Nathan M. Shippee, Chairman
THE HUMAN BEING FOUNDATION
P.O. Box 747
Old Lyme, CT 06371 USA
Nathan@humanbeingfoundation.com

FOOTNOTES

[1] Kenneth W. Miller, *Finding Darwin's God* (New York; Cliff Street Books, 1999).

[2] Dr. Francis Collins, *The New York Times*, June 26, 2000.

[3] Walt Whitman, *Democratic Vistas*

[4] Ibid.

[5] Lucien Price, *Litany for All Souls*, 1924

[6] Desmond Morris, *The Illustrated Naked Ape* (New York; Crown Publishers, Inc., 1967)

[7] Charles Darwin, *The Origin of Species* (6th ed. London, Oxford University Press, 1956 [originally published 1872])

[8] Charles Darwin, *The Descent of Man* (New York, A. L. Burt, 1874).

[9] F. Darwin, Life and Letters of Charles Darwin. (New York, D. Appleton, 1887. F. Darwin.

[10] Nathan M. Shippee, "Darwin Revisited" 1977.

[11] William Wadsworth Longfellow, "Psalm of Life"

[12] Nathan M. Shippee, "The Human Being" 1977

[13] *What Is Ancient Philosophy?* Pierre Hadot, The Belknap Press, 2002.

SUGGESTED READING LIST

Ardrey, Robert. *The Social Contract*. New York: Antheneum, 1970.

Arendt, Hannah. *Vol. I Thinking, Vol. II Willing*. New York: Harcourt Brace, 1978.

Bronowski, J. *The Ascent of Man*. Boston: Little Brown, 1973.

Bronowski, J. *A Sense of the Future*. Cambridge: MIT Press, 1977.

deChardin, Pierre Telhard. *The Phenomenon of Man*. New York: Harper Row, 1959.

Dyson, Freeman. *Disturbing the Universe*. New York: Harper & Row, 1979.

Eckstein, Gustav. *The Body has a Head*. New York: Harper & Row, 1969.

Fuller, Buckminster. *And it Came to Pass — Not to Stay*. New York: Macmillian   Publishing, 1976.

Hawking, S. *A Brief History of Time*. New York: Bantam Books, 1988.

Hoffer, Eric. *The Temper of our Time*. New York: Harper & Row, 1967.

Jaynes, Julian. *The Origin of Consciousness in the Breakdown of the Bicameral Mind*. Boston: Houghton Mifflin Co., 1976.

Jung, C.G. *Modern Man in Search of a Soul*. New York: Harcourt Brace Co., 1955.

Nouy, Lecomte du. *The Road to Reason*. New York: Longmans Green Co., 1949.

Ring, Kenneth. *Heading Toward Omega*. New York: William Morrow, 1984.

Siler, Todd. *Breaking the Mind Barrier*. New York: Simon & Schuster, 1990.

Taylor, Gordon. *The Great Evolution Mystery*. New York: Harper & Row, 1982.

Toffler, Alvin. *The Third Wave*. New York: Wm Morris & Co., 1980.

Toynbee, Arnold. *Experiences*. New York: Oxford University Press, 1969.

Wright, Robert. *Three Scientists and Their Gods*. New York: Times Books, 1988.

Yatri. Unknown Man: *The Mysterious Birth of a New Species*. New York: Simon & Schuster, 1998.

BIBLIOGRAPHY

Aller, Catherine. *The Challenge of Pierre Teilhard de Chardin*. New York: Exposition Press, Inc., 1964.

Andrews, Donald Hatch. *The Symphony of Life*. Lee's Summit, MO: Unity Books, 1966.

Ardrey, Robert. *The Territorial Imperative*. New York: Atheneum, 1966.

Ardrey, Robert. *The Social Contract*. New York: Atheneum, 1970.

Arendt, Hannah. *The Life of The Mind, Volume I: Thinking*. New York: Harcourt Brace Jovanovich, 1971.

Arendt, Hannah. *The Life of the Mind, Volume II: Willing*. New York, Harcourt Brace Jovanovich, 1978.

Auzou, Georges. *The Word of God*. St Louis, MO., Herder Book Co., 1960.

Barrett, Paul H. *Darwin on Man*. New York, E.P. Dutton, Inc., 1974.

Berry, Lester V. *A Treasury of Biblical Quotations*. Garden City, NY: Doubleday & Company, 1972.

Boorstein, Daniel J. *The Seekers*. New York: Random House, 1998.

Boorstein, Daniel J. *The Discoverers*. New York: Vintage Books, 1983.

Boorstein, Daniel J. *The Creators*. New York: Vintage Books, 1992

Bronowski, J. *The Ascent of Man*. Boston: Little, Brown and Company, 1973.

Bronowski, J. *A Sense of the Future*. Cambridge: MIT Press, 1977.

Bruner, Jerome. *In Search of Mind*. New York: Harper & Row, Publishers, 1983.

Bry, Adelaide. *Directing The Movies of Your Mind*. New York: Harper & Row, 1976.

Collin, Rodney. *The Theory of Eternal Life*. New York: Samuel Weiser, 1974.

Cousins, Norman. *Nobel Prize Conversations*. Dallas, TX: Saybrook Publishing Company, 1985.

Cuny, Hilarie. *Ivan Pavlov*. New York: Paul S. Eriksson Inc., 1965.

Day, Clarence. *This Simian World*. New York: Alfred A. Knopf, 1936.

deChardin, Pierre Teilhard. *Letters From a Traveller*. New York: Harper & Row, 1965.

deChardin, Pierre Teilhard. *The Divine Milieu*. New York: Harper & Row, 1960.

deChardin, Pierre Teilhard. *The Making of a Mind*. New York: Harper & Row, 1961.

deChardin, Pierre Teilhard. *Hymn of the Universe*. New York: Harper & Row, 1961.

deChardin, Pierre Teilhard. *Building The Earth*. Wilkes-Barre, PA: Dimension Books, 1965.

deChardin, Pierre Teilhard. *The Future of Man*. New York: Harper & Row, 1959.

deChardin, Pierre Teilhard. *The Phenomenon of Man*. New York: Harper & Row, 1959.

Desmond, Adrian. *The Ape's Reflection*. London: Blond & Briggs, 1979.

deTerra, Helmut. *Memories of Teilhard de Chardin*. New York: Harper & Row, 1962.

Driver, Tom F. *Patterns of Grace*. San Francisco: Harper & Row, 1977.

Dyson, Freeman. *Disturbing The Universe*. New York: Harper & Row, 1979.

Eckstein, Gustav. *The Body Has A Head*. New York: Harper & Row, 1969.

Eiseley, Loren. *The Star Thrower*. New York: Times Book Company, 1978.

Farb, Peter. *Humankind*. Boston: Houghton Mifflin Company, 1978.

Ford, Arthur. *The Life Beyond Death*. New York: G. P. Putnam's Sons, 1971.

Friedman, Maurice. *Martin Buber's Life and Work, The Early Years*. New York: Elsevier-Dutton Publishing Company, 1981.

Friedman, Maurice. *Martin Buber's Life and Work, The Middle Years*. New York: E. P. Dutton, Inc., 1983.

Fuller, Buckminster. *And It Came To Pass — Not To Stay*. New York: Macmillan Publishing, 1976.

Hadingham, Evan. *Early Man and the Cosmos*. New York: Walker & Company, 1984.

Hammarskjold, Dag. *Markings*. New York: Alfred-A-Knopf, 1965.

Hawking. S. *A Brief History of Time*. New York: Bantam Books, 1988.

Heidegger, Martin. *Being And Time*. New York: Harper & Row, 1962.

Heilbroner, Robert L. *The Worldly Philosophers*. New York: Simon and Schuster, 1967.

Hoffer, Eric. *The Temper of Our Time*. New York: Harper & Row, 1967.

Hoffstein, Robert M. *The English Alphabet, An Inquiry into Its Mystical Construction*. New York: Kaedmon Publishing, 1975.

Hofstadter, Douglas R. *The Mind's I*. New York: Basic Books, Inc., 1981.

Hofstadter, Douglar R. *Godel, Escher, Bach: an Eternal Golden Braid*. New York: Basic Books, 1979.

Hofstadter, Douglar R. *Matamagical Themas*. New York: Basic Books, 1985.

Huxley, Julian. *Aldous Huxley*. New York: Harper & Row, 1965.

Jaspers, Karl. *The Great Philosophers*. New York: Harcourt, Brace & World, 1957.

Jaynes, Julian. *The Origin of Consciousness In The Breakdown Of the Bicameral Mind*. Boston: Houghton Mifflin Company, 1976.

Jung, C. G. *Psychology and Alchemy*. Princeton, NJ: Princeton University Press, 1977.

Jung, C. G. *Memories, Dreams, Reflections*. New York: Pantheon Books, 1963.

Jung, C. G. *Modern Man In Search of A Soul*. New York: Harcourt Brace & Company, 1955.

Kaufmann, Walter. *Discovering The Mind*. New York: McGraw Hill Book Company, 1980.

Koestler, Arthur. *The Act of Creation*. New York: The Macmillan Company, 1964.

Konner, Melvin. *The Tangled Web*. New York: Holton, Rinehart and Winston, 1982.

Kung, Hans. *Does God Exist?* New York: Doubleday and Company, 1980.

Kurten, Bjorn. *Not From the Apes*. New York: Pantheon Books, 1972.

Lachs, John. *The Human Search*. New York: Oxford University Press, 1981.

Liebman, Joshua Loth. *Hope For Man*. New York: Simon & Schuster, 1966.

Lukas, Mary. *Teilhard: The Man, The Priest, The Scientist*. New York: Doubleday & Company, 1977.

Microsoft. *Encarta World English Dictionary*. New York: St. Martin's Press, 1999.

Morris, Desmond. *The Naked Ape*. New York: McGraw-Hill Book Company, 1967.

Morris, Desmond. *The Human Zoo*. New York: McGraw-Hill Book Company, 1969.

Nouy, Lecomte du. *The Road to Reason*. New York: Longmans, Green and Co., 1949.

Nouy, Lecomte du. *Between Knowing and Believing*. New York: David McKay Company, 1966.

Nouy, Lecomte du. *Human Destiny*. New York: Longmans, Green and Co., 1947.

Ornstein, Robert E. *The Psychology of Consciousness*. New York: The Viking Press, 1972.

Overstreet, Harry and Bonaro. *The Mind Alive*. New York: W. W. Norton, 1954.

Overstreet, Harry and Bonaro. *The Mind Goes Forth*. New York: W. W. Norton, 1956.

Perkins, D. N. *The Mind's Best Work*. Cambridge: Harvard University Press, 1981.

Pinker, Steven. *How The Mind Works*. New York: W. W. Norton, 1977.

Raven, Charles E. *Teilhard deChardin, Scientist and Seer.* New York: Harper & Row, 1962.

Ring, Kenneth. *Heading Toward Omega.* New York: William Morrow and Company, 1984.

Rorty, Amelie Oksenberg. *Mind In Action.* Boston: Beacon Press, 1988.

Sagan, Carl. *Broca's Brain.* New York: Random House, 1979.

Sagan, Carl. *The Cosmic Connection.* New York: Anchor Press, 1973.

Sagan, Carl. *The Dragons of Eden.* New York: Random House, 1977.

Shapley, Harlow. *Beyond the Observatory.* New York: Charles Scribner's Sons, 1967.

Siler, Todd. *Breaking The Mind Barrier.* New York: Simon & Schuster, 1990.

Singer, Isaac Beshevis. *Old Love.* New York: Farrar, Straus, Giroux, 1979.

Singer, Peter. *The Expanding Circle.* New York: Farrar, Straus, Giroux, 1981.

Skinner, B. F. *Beyond Freedom and Dignity.* New York: Alfred A. Knopf, 1972.

Smith, Adam. *Powers of Mind.* New York: Random House, 1975.

Smith, Anthony. *The Mind.* New York: The Viking Press, 1984.

Stone, Irving. *The Origin, A Biographical Novel of Charles Darwin*. New York: Doubleday & Company, 1980.

Taylor, Gordon Rattray. *The Great Evolution Mystery*. New York: Harper & Row, 1982.

Taylor, Gordon Rattray. *The Natural History of the Mind*. New York: A. P. Dutton, 1979.

Templeton, John M. *The Humble Approach, Scientists Discover God*. New York: The Seabury Press, 1981.

Toffler, Alvin. *Future Shock*. New York: Random House, 1970.

Toffler, Alvin. *The Third Wave*. New York: Wm. Morrow & Company, 1980.

Tonne, Herbert A. *The Human Dilemma*. New York: Prometheus Books, 1980.

Toynbee, Arnold. *Experiences*. New York: Oxford University Press, 1969.

Wilson, Edward O. *Promethean Fire*. Cambridge: Harvard University Press, 1983.

Wilson, Edward O. *On Human Nature*. Cambridge: Harvard University Press, 1978.

Wright, Robert. *Three Scientists and Their Gods*. New York: Times Books, 1988.

Yarti. Unknown Man, *The Mysterious Birth of A New Species*. New York: Simon & Schuster, 1988.

INDEX

Human Being Foundation

P.O. Box 747, Old Lyme, Connecticut 06371
Telephone: 860- 434-5108   Fax: 860-434-0366
Email: nathan@humanbeingfoundation.com

The Human Being Foundation was created to advance a philosophy designed to dignify humanity and to help people understand themselves more fully. The Human Being philosophy centers on the idea that we become as we think, and therefore our destinies may be in our own hands. The activities of the Foundation have several purposes: to educate people about the Foundation and its philosophy, to foster creativity and love and caring toward others, and to encourage community-based programs for the benevolent treatment of humanity.

"I AM A HUMAN BEING!"

About 50% of the Foundation's activities focus on the role of the Human Being in the new millennium. To that end, the Foundation sponsors the development and publication of books, musical scores, poetry, video essays, and seminars that promote the Human Being philosophy. About 35% of the Foundation's efforts support programs that focus on humanitarian aid. This includes the building and renovation of apartments and care facilities for the elderly; food and clothing drives for the impoverished and homeless; special activities for children, such as visits to nursing facilities, and job training seminars for the disadvantaged. The balance of the Foundation's activities supports creative and performing arts programs in public and private schools, as well as to encourage awareness of the Human Being philosophy. The Foundation also supports a program to encourage publishers to include the listing "Human Being" (with appropriate capitalization) in their dictionaries, as a term of respect for our species.

Because the work of the Human Being Foundation requires a great deal of support, we welcome the help and contributions of all. Please donate to the Foundation, to help restore the dignity of the disadvantaged and promote understanding, tolerance, and education for all.

THE HUMAN BEING PETITION

I, the undersigned, do hereby register my support for inclusion of the term, "Human Being," with capital H and B, in dictionaries and all other appropriate reference sources. The term Human Being, with its proper capitalization, gives dignity and recognition to what it means to be human. It is time for reference sources to acknowledge the use of this term and all it stands for, for it is a bona fide product of the evolution of language.

Signature _____

Date _____

Please copy this petition and pass it on to your friends, family and co-workers. Send your completed petition to The Human Being Foundation, P.O. Box 747, Old Lyme, Connecticut 06371 USA. If you wish to register via our web site, you may do so at Nathan@humanbeingfoundation.com. Thank you for your support.